50 Island Lunch Recipes for Home

By: Kelly Johnson

Table of Contents

- Coconut Shrimp Tacos
- Jerk Chicken Wraps
- Pineapple Chicken Skewers
- Caribbean Fish Cakes
- Tropical Quinoa Salad
- Mango Salsa Chicken
- Island-Style Beef Patties
- Ahi Poke Bowl
- Plantain and Black Bean Burritos
- Spicy Tuna Salad
- Coconut Curry Shrimp
- Jerk Pork Sliders
- Pineapple and Ham Sandwiches
- Grilled Mahi-Mahi with Lime
- Island Veggie Stir-Fry
- Barbados Beef Stew
- Spicy Jerk Chicken Quesadillas
- Pineapple Fried Rice
- Coconut Lime Chicken Salad
- Roasted Red Pepper and Mango Soup
- Calypso Crab Cakes
- Tropical Chicken and Rice
- Pineapple Guacamole with Tortilla Chips
- Curry Goat Wraps
- Sweet and Sour Shrimp Stir-Fry
- Caribbean Bean Salad
- Coconut-Crusted Fish Tacos
- Roasted Plantain and Avocado Salad
- Island-Style BBQ Ribs
- Spiced Sweet Potato and Black Bean Burritos
- Mango and Chicken Lettuce Wraps
- Spicy Caribbean Meatballs

- Coconut Milk Chicken Soup
- Jamaican Beef and Cheese Patties
- Pineapple Salsa Chicken Enchiladas
- Tropical Pork and Pineapple Skewers
- Coconut and Lime Seafood Pasta
- Grilled Chicken and Pineapple Salad
- Jerk Tempeh Wraps
- Caribbean Shrimp and Grits
- Island-style Couscous Salad
- Tropical Chicken Lettuce Cups
- Coconut Lime Shrimp Tacos
- Plantain and Chicken Stew
- Spicy Fish Tacos with Pineapple Slaw
- Jamaican Jerk Turkey Burgers
- Pineapple and Mango Chicken Skewers
- Tropical Black Bean Soup
- Grilled Fish Sandwiches with Mango Chutney
- Caribbean Chicken and Pineapple Stir-Fry

Coconut Shrimp Tacos

Ingredients:

For the Coconut Shrimp:

- 1 pound large shrimp, peeled and deveined
- 1/2 cup all-purpose flour
- 2 large eggs
- 1 cup shredded coconut
- 1 cup panko breadcrumbs
- 1/2 teaspoon salt
- 1/4 teaspoon black pepper
- Vegetable oil, for frying

For the Tacos:

- 8 small tortillas (corn or flour)
- 1 cup shredded cabbage
- 1/2 cup diced mango
- 1/4 cup chopped cilantro
- 1 lime, cut into wedges
- 1/4 cup sour cream (optional)
- 1 tablespoon lime juice (optional)
- 1 tablespoon honey (optional)

Instructions:

1. **Prepare the Shrimp:**
    - In a shallow bowl, place the flour.
    - In a second shallow bowl, beat the eggs.
    - In a third shallow bowl, combine the shredded coconut and panko breadcrumbs.
    - Dredge each shrimp in flour, shaking off the excess.
    - Dip in the beaten eggs, allowing any excess to drip off.
    - Coat with the coconut-panko mixture, pressing gently to adhere.
2. **Cook the Shrimp:**
    - Heat vegetable oil in a large skillet over medium-high heat.
    - Fry the shrimp in batches, cooking for about 2-3 minutes per side, or until golden brown and crispy.
    - Transfer cooked shrimp to a paper towel-lined plate to drain excess oil.
3. **Assemble the Tacos:**
    - Warm the tortillas in a dry skillet or microwave.
    - Spread a layer of shredded cabbage on each tortilla.
    - Top with coconut shrimp, diced mango, and chopped cilantro.

4. **Add Optional Toppings:**
    - In a small bowl, mix sour cream with lime juice and honey, if using.
    - Drizzle over tacos if desired.
5. **Serve:**
    - Serve tacos with lime wedges on the side for squeezing over the top.

Enjoy your tropical coconut shrimp tacos!

Jerk Chicken Wraps

Ingredients:

For the Jerk Chicken:

- 1 lb chicken breasts or thighs, boneless and skinless
- 2 tablespoons jerk seasoning (store-bought or homemade)
- 1 tablespoon olive oil
- 1 tablespoon lime juice
- 1 tablespoon soy sauce
- 2 cloves garlic, minced
- 1 teaspoon fresh ginger, grated

For the Wraps:

- 4 large tortillas or flatbreads
- 1 cup shredded lettuce
- 1/2 cup diced tomatoes
- 1/2 cup shredded cheese (cheddar or your choice)
- 1/4 cup thinly sliced red onion
- 1/4 cup sliced bell peppers (any color)
- 1 avocado, sliced
- 1/4 cup chopped fresh cilantro (optional)

For the Sauce (optional):

- 1/2 cup sour cream or Greek yogurt
- 1 tablespoon lime juice
- 1 tablespoon honey
- 1 teaspoon jerk seasoning

Instructions:

1. **Marinate the Chicken:**
    - In a bowl, combine jerk seasoning, olive oil, lime juice, soy sauce, garlic, and ginger.
    - Add chicken breasts or thighs to the marinade and coat evenly.
    - Cover and refrigerate for at least 30 minutes, or up to overnight for more flavor.
2. **Cook the Chicken:**
    - Preheat your grill or stovetop grill pan over medium-high heat.
    - Grill the chicken for 6-7 minutes per side, or until fully cooked and the internal temperature reaches 165°F (75°C).
    - Remove from the grill and let rest for 5 minutes before slicing into strips.

3. **Prepare the Wraps:**
   - Warm the tortillas or flatbreads in a dry skillet or microwave.
   - Place the warm tortillas on a flat surface.
4. **Assemble the Wraps:**
   - Lay a bed of shredded lettuce in the center of each tortilla.
   - Top with grilled jerk chicken strips.
   - Add diced tomatoes, shredded cheese, red onion, bell peppers, and avocado slices.
   - Sprinkle with chopped cilantro, if using.
5. **Add Sauce (Optional):**
   - In a small bowl, mix sour cream or Greek yogurt with lime juice, honey, and jerk seasoning.
   - Drizzle over the chicken and vegetables in the wrap, or serve on the side.
6. **Wrap and Serve:**
   - Fold in the sides of the tortilla and then roll it up tightly from the bottom.
   - Slice in half if desired and serve immediately.

Enjoy your spicy and flavorful jerk chicken wraps!

Pineapple Chicken Skewers

Ingredients:

For the Chicken Marinade:

- 1 lb chicken breasts or thighs, cut into bite-sized pieces
- 1/4 cup soy sauce
- 2 tablespoons honey
- 2 tablespoons olive oil
- 2 tablespoons lime juice
- 2 cloves garlic, minced
- 1 teaspoon fresh ginger, grated
- 1/2 teaspoon ground cumin
- 1/2 teaspoon paprika
- 1/4 teaspoon black pepper

For the Skewers:

- 1 cup fresh pineapple chunks (or canned, drained)
- 1 red bell pepper, cut into bite-sized pieces
- 1 yellow bell pepper, cut into bite-sized pieces
- 1 small red onion, cut into chunks
- Fresh cilantro, chopped (for garnish, optional)
- Lime wedges (for serving)

Instructions:

1. **Marinate the Chicken:**
    - In a bowl, combine soy sauce, honey, olive oil, lime juice, garlic, ginger, cumin, paprika, and black pepper.
    - Add the chicken pieces and toss to coat.
    - Cover and refrigerate for at least 30 minutes, or up to 2 hours for more flavor.
2. **Prepare the Skewers:**
    - Soak wooden skewers in water for at least 30 minutes to prevent burning, or use metal skewers.
    - Thread the marinated chicken pieces onto the skewers, alternating with pineapple chunks, bell peppers, and red onion.
3. **Grill the Skewers:**
    - Preheat your grill to medium-high heat.
    - Lightly oil the grill grates or use a grill pan.
    - Grill the skewers for 8-10 minutes, turning occasionally, until the chicken is cooked through and has nice grill marks. The internal temperature of the chicken should reach 165°F (75°C).

4. **Serve:**
    - Transfer the skewers to a serving platter.
    - Garnish with chopped fresh cilantro, if desired.
    - Serve with lime wedges on the side for a fresh squeeze of lime juice.

Enjoy your tropical and flavorful pineapple chicken skewers!

Caribbean Fish Cakes

Ingredients:

For the Fish Cakes:

- 1 lb (450g) fresh white fish fillets (such as cod or snapper), cooked and flaked
- 1 cup all-purpose flour
- 1/2 cup breadcrumbs (preferably fresh)
- 1/4 cup finely chopped onion
- 1/4 cup finely chopped bell pepper (any color)
- 2 cloves garlic, minced
- 1 teaspoon fresh thyme leaves (or 1/2 teaspoon dried thyme)
- 1 teaspoon paprika
- 1/2 teaspoon ground cumin
- 1/2 teaspoon salt
- 1/4 teaspoon black pepper
- 1 large egg, beaten
- 1 tablespoon chopped fresh parsley (optional)
- Vegetable oil, for frying

For the Spicy Dipping Sauce (optional):

- 1/4 cup mayonnaise
- 1 tablespoon hot sauce (adjust to taste)
- 1 tablespoon lime juice
- 1 teaspoon honey
- Salt and pepper, to taste

Instructions:

1. **Prepare the Fish:**
   - If using raw fish, cook it by baking, poaching, or grilling until fully cooked. Allow it to cool and then flake into small pieces.
   - If using pre-cooked fish, ensure it is thoroughly flaked and free of bones.
2. **Mix the Ingredients:**
   - In a large bowl, combine the flaked fish, flour, breadcrumbs, chopped onion, bell pepper, garlic, thyme, paprika, cumin, salt, and black pepper.
   - Add the beaten egg and mix until well combined. The mixture should be moist but firm enough to form into patties. If too dry, add a little water; if too wet, add more breadcrumbs.
3. **Shape the Fish Cakes:**
   - Form the mixture into small patties or cakes, about 2 inches in diameter and 1/2 inch thick.

4. **Fry the Fish Cakes:**
   - Heat a generous amount of vegetable oil in a large skillet over medium heat.
   - Fry the fish cakes in batches, without crowding the pan, for about 3-4 minutes per side, or until golden brown and crispy.
   - Transfer the cooked fish cakes to a paper towel-lined plate to drain excess oil.
5. **Prepare the Dipping Sauce (Optional):**
   - In a small bowl, combine mayonnaise, hot sauce, lime juice, honey, salt, and pepper. Mix well.
6. **Serve:**
   - Serve the fish cakes warm with the spicy dipping sauce on the side, or with a side of your choice such as a fresh salad or rice.

Enjoy your Caribbean Fish Cakes with their vibrant flavors and crisp texture!

Tropical Quinoa Salad

Ingredients:

For the Salad:

- 1 cup quinoa
- 2 cups water or vegetable broth
- 1 cup fresh pineapple, diced
- 1 red bell pepper, diced
- 1/2 cup diced cucumber
- 1/4 cup finely chopped red onion
- 1/4 cup chopped fresh cilantro
- 1/4 cup chopped fresh mint (optional)
- 1 avocado, diced

For the Dressing:

- 1/4 cup extra virgin olive oil
- 2 tablespoons lime juice (about 1 lime)
- 1 tablespoon honey or agave syrup
- 1 teaspoon grated ginger
- 1 clove garlic, minced
- Salt and pepper, to taste

Instructions:

1. **Cook the Quinoa:**
    - Rinse the quinoa under cold water.
    - In a medium saucepan, combine quinoa and water or vegetable broth. Bring to a boil.
    - Reduce heat to low, cover, and simmer for 15 minutes or until quinoa is tender and the liquid is absorbed.
    - Remove from heat and let it sit, covered, for 5 minutes. Fluff with a fork and let it cool to room temperature.
2. **Prepare the Salad Ingredients:**
    - In a large bowl, combine the cooled quinoa, pineapple, red bell pepper, cucumber, red onion, cilantro, mint (if using), and avocado.
3. **Make the Dressing:**
    - In a small bowl or jar, whisk together the olive oil, lime juice, honey or agave syrup, grated ginger, garlic, salt, and pepper.
4. **Combine and Serve:**
    - Pour the dressing over the salad and toss gently to combine.
    - Adjust seasoning with additional salt and pepper, if needed.

5. **Chill (Optional):**
    - For best flavor, refrigerate the salad for at least 30 minutes to allow the flavors to meld.
6. **Serve:**
    - Serve chilled or at room temperature.

Enjoy your vibrant and flavorful Tropical Quinoa Salad!

Mango Salsa Chicken

Ingredients:

For the Chicken:

- 4 boneless, skinless chicken breasts
- 2 tablespoons olive oil
- 1 teaspoon ground cumin
- 1 teaspoon paprika
- 1/2 teaspoon garlic powder
- 1/2 teaspoon onion powder
- 1/2 teaspoon salt
- 1/4 teaspoon black pepper
- 1 tablespoon lime juice

For the Mango Salsa:

- 1 ripe mango, peeled and diced
- 1/2 red bell pepper, finely diced
- 1/4 cup red onion, finely diced
- 1 small jalapeño, seeded and minced (optional, for heat)
- 1/4 cup fresh cilantro, chopped
- 1 tablespoon lime juice
- Salt and pepper, to taste

Instructions:

1. **Prepare the Chicken:**
   - Preheat your grill or oven to medium-high heat (375°F/190°C).
   - In a small bowl, mix together cumin, paprika, garlic powder, onion powder, salt, and black pepper.
   - Rub the chicken breasts with olive oil and lime juice, then coat evenly with the spice mixture.
2. **Cook the Chicken:**
   - **Grilling:** Grill the chicken for 6-8 minutes per side, or until fully cooked and the internal temperature reaches 165°F (75°C).
   - **Oven:** Place the chicken breasts on a baking sheet and bake for 20-25 minutes, or until fully cooked and the internal temperature reaches 165°F (75°C).
3. **Make the Mango Salsa:**
   - While the chicken is cooking, prepare the salsa.
   - In a bowl, combine diced mango, red bell pepper, red onion, jalapeño (if using), cilantro, and lime juice.
   - Season with salt and pepper to taste. Mix well and set aside.

4. **Serve:**
    - Once the chicken is cooked, let it rest for a few minutes before slicing.
    - Top the chicken with a generous spoonful of mango salsa.
5. **Optional Garnishes:**
    - Serve with extra lime wedges, avocado slices, or fresh cilantro for added flavor.

Enjoy your Mango Salsa Chicken, a perfect blend of savory and sweet with a tropical twist!

Island-Style Beef Patties

Ingredients:

For the Pastry Dough:

- 2 1/2 cups all-purpose flour
- 1/2 teaspoon baking powder
- 1/2 teaspoon salt
- 1/2 cup cold unsalted butter, cubed
- 1/4 cup cold water (more if needed)

For the Beef Filling:

- 1 lb (450g) ground beef
- 1 tablespoon vegetable oil
- 1 medium onion, finely chopped
- 2 cloves garlic, minced
- 1 small bell pepper, finely chopped (any color)
- 1/2 teaspoon allspice
- 1 teaspoon paprika
- 1/2 teaspoon ground cumin
- 1/2 teaspoon dried thyme
- 1/4 teaspoon cayenne pepper (optional, for heat)
- 1/2 cup beef broth
- 1/4 cup breadcrumbs
- Salt and pepper, to taste
- 1 tablespoon soy sauce
- 1 tablespoon tomato paste

For Assembly:

- 1 egg, beaten (for egg wash)

Instructions:

1. **Prepare the Pastry Dough:**
    - In a large bowl, whisk together flour, baking powder, and salt.
    - Cut in the cold butter using a pastry cutter or your fingers until the mixture resembles coarse crumbs.
    - Gradually add cold water, one tablespoon at a time, until the dough comes together.
    - Form the dough into a disk, wrap in plastic wrap, and refrigerate for at least 30 minutes.

2. **Make the Beef Filling:**
    - Heat vegetable oil in a large skillet over medium heat.
    - Add onion, garlic, and bell pepper, and sauté until softened, about 5 minutes.
    - Add ground beef and cook until browned, breaking it up with a spoon.
    - Stir in allspice, paprika, cumin, thyme, cayenne pepper (if using), salt, and pepper.
    - Add beef broth, breadcrumbs, soy sauce, and tomato paste. Mix well.
    - Simmer until the mixture is thickened and most of the liquid has evaporated, about 5-7 minutes.
    - Remove from heat and let it cool.
3. **Assemble the Patties:**
    - Preheat your oven to 375°F (190°C) and line a baking sheet with parchment paper.
    - On a floured surface, roll out the chilled dough to about 1/8-inch thickness.
    - Cut out circles of dough using a cookie cutter or a cup (about 4-5 inches in diameter).
    - Place a spoonful of the beef filling in the center of each dough circle.
    - Fold the dough over the filling to create a half-moon shape, and press the edges together to seal. Use a fork to crimp the edges for a decorative touch.
    - Brush the tops of the patties with the beaten egg.
4. **Bake the Patties:**
    - Place the patties on the prepared baking sheet.
    - Bake for 20-25 minutes, or until the pastry is golden brown and crisp.
5. **Serve:**
    - Allow the patties to cool slightly before serving.

Enjoy your Island-Style Beef Patties with their deliciously spiced beef filling and flaky pastry!

Ahi Poke Bowl

Ingredients:

For the Ahi Poke:

- 1 lb (450g) fresh ahi tuna, diced into 1/2-inch cubes (make sure it's sushi-grade)
- 1/4 cup soy sauce
- 1 tablespoon sesame oil
- 1 tablespoon rice vinegar
- 1 teaspoon honey or agave syrup
- 1 teaspoon grated ginger
- 1 clove garlic, minced
- 1-2 teaspoons sriracha (optional, for heat)
- 1 tablespoon chopped green onions
- 1 tablespoon toasted sesame seeds

For the Bowl:

- 2 cups cooked sushi rice or brown rice, warm
- 1 cup edamame, cooked and shelled
- 1 cup shredded carrots
- 1/2 cucumber, thinly sliced
- 1/2 avocado, sliced
- 1/2 cup seaweed salad (store-bought or homemade)
- 1/4 cup pickled ginger (optional)
- 1/4 cup sliced radishes (optional)
- 1 tablespoon chopped fresh cilantro (optional)

For Garnish (optional):

- Extra soy sauce
- Additional sesame seeds
- Extra sriracha or spicy mayo

Instructions:

1. **Prepare the Ahi Poke:**
   - In a medium bowl, combine soy sauce, sesame oil, rice vinegar, honey, grated ginger, minced garlic, and sriracha (if using).
   - Add the diced ahi tuna to the bowl and gently toss to coat the tuna evenly with the marinade.
   - Stir in the chopped green onions and toasted sesame seeds.
   - Cover and refrigerate while you prepare the rest of the ingredients.

2. **Assemble the Bowl:**
    - Divide the cooked rice evenly among serving bowls.
    - Arrange the edamame, shredded carrots, cucumber slices, avocado, seaweed salad, pickled ginger (if using), and radishes (if using) around the rice.
3. **Add the Ahi Poke:**
    - Spoon the marinated ahi tuna over the rice and vegetables in each bowl.
4. **Garnish and Serve:**
    - Garnish with additional sesame seeds, extra soy sauce, and a drizzle of sriracha or spicy mayo if desired.
    - Top with chopped fresh cilantro if using.
5. **Enjoy:**
    - Serve immediately for the freshest taste.

This Ahi Poke Bowl is a vibrant and nutritious meal that's packed with flavors and textures, perfect for any day of the week!

Plantain and Black Bean Burritos

Ingredients:

For the Plantains:

- 2 ripe plantains, peeled and sliced into 1/2-inch thick rounds
- 2 tablespoons olive oil
- 1/2 teaspoon ground cumin
- 1/2 teaspoon paprika
- 1/4 teaspoon salt
- 1/4 teaspoon black pepper

For the Black Bean Filling:

- 1 tablespoon olive oil
- 1 small onion, finely chopped
- 2 cloves garlic, minced
- 1 can (15 oz) black beans, drained and rinsed
- 1/2 cup corn kernels (fresh, frozen, or canned)
- 1/2 teaspoon ground cumin
- 1/2 teaspoon chili powder
- 1/4 teaspoon smoked paprika
- Salt and pepper, to taste

For Assembly:

- 4 large tortillas (flour or whole wheat)
- 1 cup cooked rice (optional, for extra filling)
- 1 cup shredded cheese (cheddar, Monterey Jack, or your choice)
- 1/2 cup salsa or pico de gallo
- 1 avocado, sliced
- 1/4 cup fresh cilantro, chopped (optional)
- Lime wedges (for serving)

Instructions:

1. **Prepare the Plantains:**
   - Preheat your oven to 400°F (200°C).
   - In a bowl, toss plantain slices with olive oil, cumin, paprika, salt, and pepper.
   - Arrange the plantain slices in a single layer on a baking sheet.
   - Bake for 20-25 minutes, flipping halfway through, until golden and tender.
2. **Make the Black Bean Filling:**
   - While the plantains are baking, heat olive oil in a skillet over medium heat.

- Add the chopped onion and cook until softened, about 5 minutes.
- Add minced garlic and cook for another 1 minute.
- Stir in the black beans, corn, cumin, chili powder, smoked paprika, salt, and pepper.
- Cook until heated through, about 5 minutes. Adjust seasoning to taste.

3. **Assemble the Burritos:**
    - Warm the tortillas in a dry skillet or microwave to make them more pliable.
    - On each tortilla, spread a layer of cooked rice (if using), then add a portion of the black bean mixture.
    - Top with baked plantain slices, shredded cheese, and salsa or pico de gallo.
    - Add avocado slices and sprinkle with fresh cilantro, if using.
4. **Wrap and Serve:**
    - Fold the sides of the tortilla in and roll up from the bottom to enclose the filling.
    - Serve the burritos warm, with lime wedges on the side for squeezing over the top.

Enjoy your Plantain and Black Bean Burritos, packed with sweet plantains and hearty black beans for a delicious and satisfying meal!

Spicy Tuna Salad

Ingredients:

For the Salad:

- 1 can (5 oz) tuna, drained (preferably packed in water or olive oil)
- 2 tablespoons mayonnaise
- 1 tablespoon Sriracha or other hot sauce (adjust to taste)
- 1 tablespoon soy sauce
- 1 teaspoon rice vinegar or lemon juice
- 1 celery stalk, finely chopped
- 1/4 cup red onion, finely chopped
- 1/4 cup chopped fresh cilantro or parsley
- 1/4 teaspoon garlic powder
- Salt and pepper, to taste

For Serving (optional):

- Lettuce leaves or salad greens
- Whole grain crackers or pita chips
- Sliced avocado
- Cherry tomatoes, halved

Instructions:

1. **Prepare the Salad:**
   - In a medium bowl, combine mayonnaise, Sriracha, soy sauce, and rice vinegar or lemon juice.
   - Add the drained tuna, celery, red onion, cilantro, and garlic powder. Gently mix until well combined.
   - Season with salt and pepper to taste.
2. **Serve:**
   - Serve the spicy tuna salad over lettuce leaves or salad greens, or enjoy it with whole grain crackers or pita chips.
   - Garnish with sliced avocado and cherry tomatoes, if desired.
3. **Chill (Optional):**
   - For best flavor, chill the salad in the refrigerator for about 30 minutes before serving to let the flavors meld.

Enjoy your spicy tuna salad with its perfect balance of heat and savory goodness!

Coconut Curry Shrimp

Ingredients:

For the Shrimp:

- 1 lb (450g) large shrimp, peeled and deveined
- 1 tablespoon olive oil or vegetable oil
- 1 onion, finely chopped
- 3 cloves garlic, minced
- 1 tablespoon fresh ginger, grated
- 1 tablespoon curry powder
- 1 teaspoon ground cumin
- 1/2 teaspoon paprika
- 1/4 teaspoon turmeric (optional, for color)
- 1 can (14 oz) coconut milk
- 1/2 cup chicken or vegetable broth
- 1 tablespoon fish sauce (optional, for umami)
- 1 tablespoon lime juice
- 1 tablespoon brown sugar or honey
- Salt and pepper, to taste
- 1/4 cup chopped fresh cilantro (for garnish)

For Serving:

- Cooked rice or quinoa
- Lime wedges
- Extra cilantro for garnish

Instructions:

1. **Cook the Aromatics:**
    - Heat the oil in a large skillet or saucepan over medium heat.
    - Add the chopped onion and cook until softened, about 5 minutes.
    - Stir in the minced garlic and grated ginger, cooking for another 1-2 minutes until fragrant.
2. **Add Spices:**
    - Stir in the curry powder, ground cumin, paprika, and turmeric (if using).
    - Cook for 1-2 minutes, stirring constantly, to toast the spices and enhance their flavors.
3. **Prepare the Sauce:**
    - Pour in the coconut milk and chicken or vegetable broth, stirring to combine.
    - Add fish sauce (if using), lime juice, and brown sugar or honey.

- Bring the mixture to a simmer, then reduce the heat and let it cook for 5-7 minutes to slightly thicken and develop flavors.
4. **Cook the Shrimp:**
    - Add the shrimp to the skillet and cook until pink and opaque, about 3-5 minutes, depending on size.
    - Season with salt and pepper to taste.
5. **Serve:**
    - Serve the coconut curry shrimp over cooked rice or quinoa.
    - Garnish with chopped fresh cilantro and lime wedges on the side.

Enjoy your creamy and flavorful Coconut Curry Shrimp!

Jerk Pork Sliders

Ingredients:

For the Jerk Pork:

- 1.5 lbs (680g) pork shoulder, trimmed and cut into small cubes
- 2 tablespoons jerk seasoning (store-bought or homemade)
- 2 tablespoons vegetable oil
- 1 medium onion, finely chopped
- 3 cloves garlic, minced
- 1/2 cup chicken or vegetable broth
- 2 tablespoons soy sauce
- 1 tablespoon brown sugar or honey
- 1 tablespoon apple cider vinegar
- 1/2 teaspoon allspice
- 1/4 teaspoon cayenne pepper (optional, for extra heat)

For the Sliders:

- 12 slider buns or small rolls
- 1 cup coleslaw (store-bought or homemade)
- 1/4 cup pickled red onions (optional)
- Fresh cilantro or parsley, chopped (for garnish, optional)

Instructions:

1. **Prepare the Jerk Pork:**
   - In a bowl, toss the pork cubes with the jerk seasoning until well coated.
   - Heat vegetable oil in a large skillet or Dutch oven over medium-high heat.
   - Add the pork cubes in batches (don't overcrowd the pan) and brown on all sides, about 5 minutes per batch. Transfer browned pork to a plate.
   - In the same skillet, add chopped onion and cook until softened, about 5 minutes.
   - Stir in minced garlic and cook for another 1 minute.
   - Return the pork to the skillet and add chicken or vegetable broth, soy sauce, brown sugar or honey, apple cider vinegar, allspice, and cayenne pepper (if using).
   - Bring to a simmer, then reduce heat to low, cover, and cook for 1.5-2 hours, or until the pork is tender and easily shredded.
2. **Shred the Pork:**
   - Once the pork is tender, use two forks to shred the meat in the skillet. Stir to combine with the sauce.
3. **Assemble the Sliders:**
   - Slice the slider buns in half and lightly toast them if desired.

- Spoon a generous amount of the jerk pork mixture onto the bottom half of each slider bun.
- Top with a spoonful of coleslaw, pickled red onions (if using), and garnish with chopped cilantro or parsley.

4. **Serve:**
    - Place the top half of the buns on each slider and serve immediately.

Enjoy your flavorful Jerk Pork Sliders with a spicy kick and a crunchy, fresh topping!

Pineapple and Ham Sandwiches

Ingredients:

For the Sandwiches:

- 8 slices of bread (your choice, such as whole grain, white, or sandwich rolls)
- 4 slices of deli ham (or more, depending on your preference)
- 4 slices of Swiss cheese (or cheddar, provolone, or your choice)
- 1/2 cup canned pineapple rings, drained and patted dry
- 2 tablespoons Dijon mustard (or mayonnaise, if preferred)
- 1 tablespoon butter (for toasting the bread)

For Garnish (optional):

- Lettuce leaves
- Sliced tomatoes
- Pickles

Instructions:

1. **Prepare the Ingredients:**
   - If using bread slices, you can lightly toast them if you prefer a bit of crunch.
2. **Assemble the Sandwiches:**
   - Spread Dijon mustard or mayonnaise on one side of each slice of bread.
   - Layer a slice of ham on top of the mustard/mayonnaise.
   - Place a slice of cheese on top of the ham.
   - Add a pineapple ring on top of the cheese.
   - If using, add any additional garnishes like lettuce or tomato.
3. **Grill or Toast the Sandwiches:**
   - Heat butter in a skillet over medium heat.
   - Place the assembled sandwiches in the skillet and cook until the bread is golden brown and the cheese is melted, about 2-3 minutes per side.
   - Press down lightly with a spatula to ensure even grilling.
4. **Serve:**
   - Remove the sandwiches from the skillet and let them cool slightly before slicing in half, if desired.
   - Serve warm with any additional sides or garnishes.

Enjoy your Pineapple and Ham Sandwiches, a sweet and savory combination that's both satisfying and easy to make!

Grilled Mahi-Mahi with Lime

Ingredients:

For the Marinade:

- 4 mahi-mahi fillets (about 6 oz each)
- 1/4 cup olive oil
- 2 tablespoons lime juice (about 1 lime)
- 2 cloves garlic, minced
- 1 tablespoon honey or agave syrup
- 1 teaspoon ground cumin
- 1/2 teaspoon smoked paprika
- 1/2 teaspoon dried oregano
- 1/4 teaspoon cayenne pepper (optional, for heat)
- Salt and black pepper, to taste

For Serving:

- Lime wedges
- Fresh cilantro, chopped (optional)
- Sliced avocado (optional)

Instructions:

1. **Prepare the Marinade:**
    - In a small bowl, whisk together olive oil, lime juice, minced garlic, honey, ground cumin, smoked paprika, dried oregano, cayenne pepper (if using), salt, and black pepper.
2. **Marinate the Mahi-Mahi:**
    - Place the mahi-mahi fillets in a shallow dish or a resealable plastic bag.
    - Pour the marinade over the fillets, making sure they are well coated.
    - Cover and refrigerate for at least 30 minutes, or up to 2 hours for more flavor.
3. **Preheat the Grill:**
    - Preheat your grill to medium-high heat (about 400°F/200°C).
    - Oil the grill grates to prevent sticking.
4. **Grill the Mahi-Mahi:**
    - Remove the mahi-mahi fillets from the marinade and discard the excess marinade.
    - Place the fillets on the grill and cook for 4-5 minutes per side, or until the fish is opaque and flakes easily with a fork.
    - Be careful not to overcook, as mahi-mahi can become dry if grilled too long.
5. **Serve:**
    - Transfer the grilled mahi-mahi to a serving platter.

- Garnish with lime wedges and chopped fresh cilantro, if desired.
- Serve with sliced avocado or your favorite side dishes, such as a fresh salad or rice.

Enjoy your Grilled Mahi-Mahi with Lime, a light and refreshing dish with vibrant flavors!

Island Veggie Stir-Fry

Ingredients:

For the Stir-Fry:

- 2 tablespoons coconut oil (or vegetable oil)
- 1 red bell pepper, sliced
- 1 yellow bell pepper, sliced
- 1 cup snap peas or snow peas
- 1 cup broccoli florets
- 1 cup baby corn (fresh or canned)
- 1 cup sliced carrots
- 1 small red onion, thinly sliced
- 2 cloves garlic, minced
- 1 tablespoon fresh ginger, minced
- 1 cup pineapple chunks (fresh or canned, drained)
- 1/4 cup chopped fresh cilantro (optional)

For the Sauce:

- 1/4 cup soy sauce or tamari (for gluten-free)
- 2 tablespoons hoisin sauce
- 1 tablespoon rice vinegar
- 1 tablespoon coconut sugar or brown sugar
- 1 teaspoon sesame oil
- 1 teaspoon cornstarch mixed with 2 tablespoons water (for thickening)

Instructions:

1. **Prepare the Sauce:**
   - In a small bowl, whisk together soy sauce, hoisin sauce, rice vinegar, coconut sugar, and sesame oil.
   - Stir in the cornstarch mixture to thicken the sauce. Set aside.
2. **Stir-Fry the Vegetables:**
   - Heat coconut oil in a large skillet or wok over medium-high heat.
   - Add sliced red and yellow bell peppers, snap peas, broccoli, baby corn, and sliced carrots. Stir-fry for about 4-5 minutes, or until the vegetables are tender-crisp.
   - Add sliced red onion, minced garlic, and minced ginger. Continue to stir-fry for another 1-2 minutes until fragrant.
3. **Add Pineapple and Sauce:**
   - Add the pineapple chunks to the skillet.
   - Pour the prepared sauce over the vegetables and pineapple.

- Stir well to coat the vegetables and pineapple with the sauce.
            - Cook for another 2-3 minutes, or until the sauce has thickened and everything is heated through.
    4. **Serve:**
        - Remove from heat and garnish with chopped fresh cilantro, if desired.
        - Serve the stir-fry over cooked rice, quinoa, or noodles.

Enjoy your vibrant and delicious Island Veggie Stir-Fry, full of tropical flavors and fresh vegetables!

Barbados Beef Stew

Ingredients:

For the Beef Stew:

- 2 lbs (900g) beef chuck or stew beef, cut into 1-inch cubes
- 2 tablespoons vegetable oil
- 1 large onion, chopped
- 4 cloves garlic, minced
- 1 tablespoon fresh ginger, grated
- 2 medium carrots, sliced
- 2 medium potatoes, peeled and diced
- 1 red bell pepper, chopped
- 1 green bell pepper, chopped
- 1 can (14 oz) diced tomatoes
- 1 cup beef broth or water
- 1 tablespoon tomato paste
- 2 tablespoons soy sauce
- 1 tablespoon brown sugar
- 1 teaspoon allspice
- 1 teaspoon dried thyme
- 1 teaspoon paprika
- 1/2 teaspoon ground cumin
- 1/4 teaspoon cayenne pepper (optional, for heat)
- 1 bay leaf
- Salt and black pepper, to taste

For Garnish (optional):

- Chopped fresh parsley or cilantro

Instructions:

1. **Brown the Beef:**
   - Heat vegetable oil in a large pot or Dutch oven over medium-high heat.
   - Add the beef cubes in batches (to avoid overcrowding) and brown on all sides, about 5-7 minutes per batch. Remove the browned beef and set aside.
2. **Cook the Aromatics:**
   - In the same pot, add chopped onion, garlic, and grated ginger. Cook until the onion is softened and translucent, about 5 minutes.
3. **Add Vegetables and Spices:**
   - Stir in the carrots, potatoes, red bell pepper, and green bell pepper.

- Add allspice, dried thyme, paprika, ground cumin, and cayenne pepper (if using). Cook for another 2 minutes, stirring occasionally.
4. **Combine Ingredients:**
   - Return the browned beef to the pot.
   - Stir in the diced tomatoes, beef broth, tomato paste, soy sauce, and brown sugar. Add the bay leaf.
   - Season with salt and black pepper to taste.
5. **Simmer the Stew:**
   - Bring the mixture to a boil, then reduce heat to low.
   - Cover and simmer for 1.5 to 2 hours, or until the beef is tender and the vegetables are cooked through. Stir occasionally.
6. **Finish and Serve:**
   - Remove the bay leaf before serving.
   - Garnish with chopped fresh parsley or cilantro, if desired.

Serve the Barbados Beef Stew with rice, bread, or over mashed potatoes for a hearty and satisfying meal. Enjoy the rich flavors and comforting texture of this Caribbean-inspired stew!

Spicy Jerk Chicken Quesadillas

Ingredients:

For the Jerk Chicken:

- 1 lb (450g) boneless, skinless chicken breasts or thighs
- 2 tablespoons jerk seasoning (store-bought or homemade)
- 1 tablespoon olive oil
- 1 tablespoon soy sauce
- 1 tablespoon lime juice

For the Quesadillas:

- 4 large flour tortillas
- 1 cup shredded mozzarella cheese
- 1 cup shredded cheddar cheese
- 1/2 cup finely chopped red bell pepper
- 1/2 cup finely chopped red onion
- 1/4 cup chopped fresh cilantro (optional)
- 1 tablespoon olive oil (for cooking)

For Serving (optional):

- Salsa
- Sour cream
- Sliced jalapeños
- Lime wedges

Instructions:

1. **Prepare the Jerk Chicken:**
    - In a bowl, toss the chicken with jerk seasoning, olive oil, soy sauce, and lime juice. Let it marinate for at least 30 minutes, or up to 2 hours in the refrigerator for more flavor.
2. **Cook the Chicken:**
    - Heat a grill pan or skillet over medium-high heat. Cook the marinated chicken for 5-7 minutes per side, or until fully cooked and the internal temperature reaches 165°F (74°C).
    - Remove the chicken from the pan and let it rest for a few minutes before slicing or shredding.
3. **Prepare the Quesadilla Filling:**
    - In a bowl, combine the shredded mozzarella and cheddar cheeses. Add the finely chopped red bell pepper and red onion. Mix well.

4. **Assemble the Quesadillas:**
    - Heat a large skillet or griddle over medium heat and lightly brush with olive oil.
    - Place one tortilla in the skillet and sprinkle half of the cheese mixture evenly over the tortilla.
    - Add a layer of sliced or shredded jerk chicken on top of the cheese.
    - Sprinkle with a bit more cheese, if desired, and top with a second tortilla.
5. **Cook the Quesadillas:**
    - Cook for about 2-3 minutes on each side, or until the tortillas are golden brown and the cheese is melted. Press down with a spatula to ensure even cooking and a good seal.
    - Remove from the skillet and let cool slightly before cutting into wedges.
6. **Serve:**
    - Serve the quesadillas with salsa, sour cream, sliced jalapeños, and lime wedges on the side.

Enjoy your Spicy Jerk Chicken Quesadillas, combining the spicy, aromatic flavors of jerk seasoning with the gooey goodness of cheese and the crispy tortilla!

Pineapple Fried Rice

Ingredients:

For the Fried Rice:

- 2 cups cooked jasmine rice or basmati rice (preferably cold or day-old for better texture)
- 1 cup fresh pineapple chunks (or canned pineapple, drained)
- 2 tablespoons vegetable oil or coconut oil
- 1 small onion, chopped
- 2 cloves garlic, minced
- 1 small red bell pepper, chopped
- 1 cup frozen peas and carrots (or fresh if preferred)
- 2 green onions, sliced
- 2 large eggs, lightly beaten
- 2-3 tablespoons soy sauce (adjust to taste)
- 1 tablespoon oyster sauce (optional)
- 1 teaspoon sesame oil (optional)
- 1/2 teaspoon ground black pepper
- 1/4 teaspoon red pepper flakes (optional, for heat)

For Garnish (optional):

- Chopped fresh cilantro
- Extra pineapple chunks
- Sliced green onions
- Lime wedges

Instructions:

1. **Prepare the Ingredients:**
    - If using day-old rice, break up any clumps. If cooking rice fresh, allow it to cool completely before using for best results.
2. **Cook the Vegetables:**
    - Heat vegetable oil or coconut oil in a large skillet or wok over medium-high heat.
    - Add chopped onion and cook until softened, about 3-4 minutes.
    - Stir in minced garlic and cook for another 30 seconds until fragrant.
    - Add chopped red bell pepper and cook for 2-3 minutes until slightly tender.
    - Add frozen peas and carrots (or fresh) and cook until heated through.
3. **Add Pineapple and Rice:**
    - Stir in pineapple chunks and cook for another 1-2 minutes.
    - Push the vegetables to one side of the skillet, add a little more oil if needed, and pour the beaten eggs into the empty side.
    - Scramble the eggs until fully cooked, then mix them with the vegetables.

4. **Add the Rice:**
    - Add the cold rice to the skillet. Use a spatula to break up any clumps and stir to combine with the vegetables and eggs.
5. **Season and Finish:**
    - Stir in soy sauce, oyster sauce (if using), sesame oil (if using), black pepper, and red pepper flakes (if using).
    - Continue to stir-fry for another 2-3 minutes, allowing the flavors to meld and the rice to heat through.
6. **Serve:**
    - Garnish with chopped fresh cilantro, extra pineapple chunks, and sliced green onions if desired.
    - Serve with lime wedges on the side for an extra burst of freshness.

Enjoy your Pineapple Fried Rice, a delightful combination of sweet, savory, and tangy flavors that make for a refreshing and satisfying dish!

Coconut Lime Chicken Salad

Ingredients:

For the Chicken Salad:

- 2 cups cooked chicken breast, diced or shredded (grilled, poached, or rotisserie)
- 1 cup shredded coconut (unsweetened or sweetened, depending on your preference)
- 1 cup sliced red bell pepper
- 1 cup diced cucumber
- 1/2 cup shredded carrots
- 1/4 cup finely chopped red onion
- 1/4 cup chopped fresh cilantro
- 1/4 cup chopped fresh mint (optional)

For the Coconut Lime Dressing:

- 1/4 cup coconut milk (full-fat or light)
- 2 tablespoons lime juice (about 1 lime)
- 1 tablespoon honey or agave syrup
- 1 tablespoon soy sauce or tamari (for gluten-free)
- 1 teaspoon sesame oil (optional)
- 1 clove garlic, minced
- Salt and black pepper, to taste

Instructions:

1. **Prepare the Chicken Salad:**
   - In a large bowl, combine diced or shredded chicken, shredded coconut, sliced red bell pepper, diced cucumber, shredded carrots, red onion, cilantro, and mint (if using).
2. **Make the Coconut Lime Dressing:**
   - In a small bowl or jar, whisk together coconut milk, lime juice, honey, soy sauce, sesame oil (if using), and minced garlic.
   - Season with salt and black pepper to taste.
3. **Combine and Serve:**
   - Pour the dressing over the chicken and vegetable mixture.
   - Gently toss to coat all the ingredients evenly with the dressing.
   - Adjust seasoning with more salt and pepper if needed.
4. **Chill (Optional):**
   - For best flavor, chill the salad in the refrigerator for at least 30 minutes before serving to let the flavors meld.
5. **Serve:**

- Serve the Coconut Lime Chicken Salad on a bed of greens, in lettuce wraps, or with your favorite crackers or pita bread.

Enjoy your Coconut Lime Chicken Salad, a light and tropical meal that's bursting with fresh flavors and vibrant textures!

Roasted Red Pepper and Mango Soup

Ingredients:

For the Chicken Salad:

- 2 cups cooked chicken breast, diced or shredded (grilled, poached, or rotisserie)
- 1 cup shredded coconut (unsweetened or sweetened, depending on your preference)
- 1 cup sliced red bell pepper
- 1 cup diced cucumber
- 1/2 cup shredded carrots
- 1/4 cup finely chopped red onion
- 1/4 cup chopped fresh cilantro
- 1/4 cup chopped fresh mint (optional)

For the Coconut Lime Dressing:

- 1/4 cup coconut milk (full-fat or light)
- 2 tablespoons lime juice (about 1 lime)
- 1 tablespoon honey or agave syrup
- 1 tablespoon soy sauce or tamari (for gluten-free)
- 1 teaspoon sesame oil (optional)
- 1 clove garlic, minced
- Salt and black pepper, to taste

Instructions:

1. **Prepare the Chicken Salad:**
    - In a large bowl, combine diced or shredded chicken, shredded coconut, sliced red bell pepper, diced cucumber, shredded carrots, red onion, cilantro, and mint (if using).
2. **Make the Coconut Lime Dressing:**
    - In a small bowl or jar, whisk together coconut milk, lime juice, honey, soy sauce, sesame oil (if using), and minced garlic.
    - Season with salt and black pepper to taste.
3. **Combine and Serve:**
    - Pour the dressing over the chicken and vegetable mixture.
    - Gently toss to coat all the ingredients evenly with the dressing.
    - Adjust seasoning with more salt and pepper if needed.
4. **Chill (Optional):**
    - For best flavor, chill the salad in the refrigerator for at least 30 minutes before serving to let the flavors meld.
5. **Serve:**

- Serve the Coconut Lime Chicken Salad on a bed of greens, in lettuce wraps, or with your favorite crackers or pita bread.

Enjoy your Coconut Lime Chicken Salad, a light and tropical meal that's bursting with fresh flavors and vibrant textures!

Roasted Red Pepper and Mango Soup

Ingredients:

For the Soup:

- 4 large red bell peppers
- 1 tablespoon olive oil
- 1 medium onion, chopped
- 3 cloves garlic, minced
- 1 teaspoon ground cumin
- 1/2 teaspoon smoked paprika
- 1/4 teaspoon ground turmeric (optional)
- 1 ripe mango, peeled, pitted, and diced
- 4 cups vegetable broth or chicken broth
- 1 (14 oz) can diced tomatoes
- 1 tablespoon balsamic vinegar or apple cider vinegar
- Salt and black pepper, to taste
- 1/4 cup heavy cream or coconut milk (optional, for a creamier texture)

For Garnish (optional):

- Chopped fresh cilantro
- Croutons or toasted bread
- A swirl of cream or coconut milk

Instructions:

1. **Roast the Red Peppers:**
    - Preheat your oven to 450°F (230°C).
    - Place the whole red bell peppers on a baking sheet and roast for 20-25 minutes, turning occasionally, until the skin is blackened and blistered.
    - Transfer the peppers to a bowl and cover with plastic wrap. Let them steam for 10 minutes.
    - Peel off the skins, remove the seeds, and roughly chop the peppers. Set aside.
2. **Cook the Soup Base:**
    - In a large pot, heat olive oil over medium heat.
    - Add chopped onion and cook until softened and translucent, about 5 minutes.
    - Stir in minced garlic, ground cumin, smoked paprika, and turmeric (if using). Cook for another 1-2 minutes until fragrant.
3. **Combine Ingredients:**
    - Add the roasted red peppers, diced mango, vegetable broth, diced tomatoes, and balsamic vinegar to the pot.

- Bring to a boil, then reduce heat and simmer for 10 minutes, allowing the flavors to meld.
4. **Blend the Soup:**
   - Use an immersion blender to blend the soup until smooth. Alternatively, carefully transfer the soup in batches to a blender and blend until smooth.
   - If using a blender, return the soup to the pot after blending.
5. **Finish and Serve:**
   - Stir in the heavy cream or coconut milk if desired for a creamier texture.
   - Season with salt and black pepper to taste.
6. **Garnish (Optional):**
   - Serve the soup hot, garnished with chopped fresh cilantro, croutons, or a swirl of cream or coconut milk.

Enjoy your Roasted Red Pepper and Mango Soup, a vibrant and flavorful soup with a delightful combination of sweet and savory notes!

Calypso Crab Cakes

Ingredients:

For the Crab Cakes:

- 1 lb (450g) lump crab meat (fresh or canned, drained)
- 1/2 cup breadcrumbs (plain or panko)
- 1/4 cup finely chopped red bell pepper
- 1/4 cup finely chopped green bell pepper
- 1/4 cup finely chopped green onions
- 1/4 cup finely chopped fresh cilantro
- 1 large egg
- 1 tablespoon mayonnaise
- 1 tablespoon Dijon mustard
- 1 teaspoon jerk seasoning (adjust to taste)
- 1/2 teaspoon ground cumin
- 1/4 teaspoon cayenne pepper (optional, for extra heat)
- Salt and black pepper, to taste
- 2 tablespoons vegetable oil (for frying)

For the Lime Aioli (optional):

- 1/2 cup mayonnaise
- 2 tablespoons lime juice
- 1 teaspoon lime zest
- 1 clove garlic, minced
- Salt and black pepper, to taste

Instructions:

1. **Prepare the Crab Cake Mixture:**
    - In a large bowl, gently combine the crab meat, breadcrumbs, red and green bell peppers, green onions, and cilantro.
    - In a separate small bowl, whisk together the egg, mayonnaise, Dijon mustard, jerk seasoning, ground cumin, cayenne pepper (if using), salt, and black pepper.
    - Pour the egg mixture over the crab mixture and gently fold together until well combined. Be careful not to break up the crab meat too much.
2. **Form the Crab Cakes:**
    - Shape the mixture into 8-10 patties, about 1/2 inch thick.
    - Place the patties on a baking sheet or plate and refrigerate for at least 30 minutes to help them hold their shape during cooking.
3. **Cook the Crab Cakes:**
    - Heat vegetable oil in a large skillet over medium heat.

- Add the crab cakes to the skillet (in batches if necessary to avoid overcrowding) and cook for 3-4 minutes per side, or until golden brown and crispy. Flip gently with a spatula.
4. **Prepare the Lime Aioli (optional):**
    - In a small bowl, combine mayonnaise, lime juice, lime zest, minced garlic, salt, and black pepper. Mix well until smooth.
5. **Serve:**
    - Serve the crab cakes warm, with a dollop of lime aioli if desired.
    - They can be served as an appetizer, with a side salad, or as a main dish with rice or tropical fruit salsa.

Enjoy your Calypso Crab Cakes, bursting with Caribbean flavors and complemented by a zesty lime aioli!

Tropical Chicken and Rice

Ingredients:

For the Chicken:

- 1.5 lbs (680g) boneless, skinless chicken thighs or breasts, cut into bite-sized pieces
- 2 tablespoons olive oil
- 1 teaspoon ground cumin
- 1 teaspoon paprika
- 1/2 teaspoon turmeric
- 1/2 teaspoon garlic powder
- 1/2 teaspoon onion powder
- 1/4 teaspoon cayenne pepper (optional, for extra heat)
- Salt and black pepper, to taste

For the Rice:

- 1 cup long-grain white rice or jasmine rice
- 1 1/2 cups chicken broth
- 1/2 cup canned coconut milk (full-fat or light)
- 1/2 teaspoon ground turmeric (for color, optional)
- 1 cup fresh pineapple chunks (or canned, drained)
- 1/2 cup diced red bell pepper
- 1/4 cup chopped fresh cilantro (for garnish)

For Garnish (optional):

- Lime wedges
- Extra chopped cilantro
- Sliced green onions

Instructions:

1. **Prepare the Chicken:**
    - In a large bowl, toss the chicken pieces with olive oil, ground cumin, paprika, turmeric, garlic powder, onion powder, cayenne pepper (if using), salt, and black pepper.
    - Heat a large skillet or Dutch oven over medium-high heat.
    - Add the seasoned chicken and cook until browned on all sides and cooked through, about 6-8 minutes. Remove the chicken from the skillet and set aside.
2. **Prepare the Rice:**
    - In the same skillet, add a little more oil if needed and sauté any remaining spices and flavors from the chicken for about 1 minute.

- Stir in the rice and cook for 1-2 minutes, allowing it to toast slightly.
    - Add the chicken broth, coconut milk, and ground turmeric (if using) to the skillet. Stir to combine and bring to a boil.
3. **Combine Ingredients:**
    - Reduce heat to low, cover, and simmer for about 15 minutes, or until the rice is tender and the liquid is absorbed.
    - Gently fold in the fresh pineapple chunks and diced red bell pepper.
    - Return the cooked chicken to the skillet and stir to combine with the rice. Cover and cook for an additional 5 minutes, allowing the flavors to meld and the pineapple and bell pepper to warm through.
4. **Serve:**
    - Garnish with chopped fresh cilantro, lime wedges, and extra sliced green onions if desired.

Enjoy your Tropical Chicken and Rice, a delightful blend of savory chicken, fragrant rice, and sweet tropical fruit for a refreshing and satisfying meal!

Pineapple Guacamole with Tortilla Chips

Ingredients:

For the Pineapple Guacamole:

- 2 ripe avocados
- 1 cup fresh pineapple chunks (diced)
- 1/2 small red onion, finely chopped
- 1 small tomato, diced
- 1 small jalapeño, seeds removed and finely chopped (optional, for heat)
- 2 tablespoons fresh lime juice (about 1 lime)
- 2 tablespoons chopped fresh cilantro
- Salt and black pepper, to taste

For the Tortilla Chips:

- 8-10 corn tortillas
- 1/4 cup vegetable oil or coconut oil
- 1/2 teaspoon salt (or to taste)
- 1/2 teaspoon chili powder (optional, for extra flavor)

Instructions:

1. **Prepare the Tortilla Chips:**
   - Preheat your oven to 375°F (190°C).
   - Cut the corn tortillas into wedges (eighths work well) and place them on a baking sheet.
   - Brush or lightly spray the tortilla wedges with vegetable oil or coconut oil.
   - Sprinkle with salt and chili powder if using.
   - Bake for 10-15 minutes, or until the chips are crispy and golden brown. Keep an eye on them to avoid burning. Allow to cool completely.
2. **Prepare the Pineapple Guacamole:**
   - Cut the avocados in half, remove the pits, and scoop the flesh into a mixing bowl.
   - Mash the avocados with a fork until smooth but still slightly chunky.
   - Gently fold in the diced pineapple, chopped red onion, diced tomato, jalapeño (if using), lime juice, and chopped cilantro.
   - Season with salt and black pepper to taste.
3. **Serve:**
   - Transfer the Pineapple Guacamole to a serving bowl.
   - Serve immediately with the homemade tortilla chips on the side.

Enjoy your Pineapple Guacamole with Tortilla Chips, a perfect blend of creamy, tangy, and sweet flavors with a satisfying crunch!

Curry Goat Wraps

Ingredients:

For the Curry Goat:

- 2 lbs (900g) goat meat, cut into bite-sized pieces (can substitute with beef if goat is unavailable)
- 2 tablespoons curry powder
- 1 tablespoon allspice
- 1 teaspoon ground cumin
- 1 teaspoon paprika
- 1/2 teaspoon turmeric
- 1 teaspoon garlic powder
- 1 teaspoon onion powder
- 1/2 teaspoon cayenne pepper (optional, for extra heat)
- 2 tablespoons vegetable oil
- 1 large onion, chopped
- 4 cloves garlic, minced
- 1 thumb-sized piece of fresh ginger, grated
- 1-2 Scotch bonnet peppers, chopped (seeds removed for less heat)
- 1 large tomato, chopped
- 1 cup beef or vegetable broth
- 1 tablespoon tomato paste
- 1 tablespoon soy sauce or tamari
- 1-2 tablespoons brown sugar (adjust to taste)
- Salt and black pepper, to taste
- 1-2 tablespoons fresh lime juice

For the Wraps:

- 4 large flour tortillas or flatbreads
- 1 cup shredded lettuce or cabbage
- 1/2 cup diced tomatoes
- 1/2 cup thinly sliced red onion
- 1/2 cup sliced cucumber
- 1/4 cup chopped fresh cilantro
- 1/4 cup sour cream or Greek yogurt (optional)
- Lime wedges (for serving)

Instructions:

1. **Prepare the Curry Goat:**

- In a large bowl, mix the goat meat with curry powder, allspice, cumin, paprika, turmeric, garlic powder, onion powder, and cayenne pepper (if using). Let it marinate for at least 30 minutes, or up to overnight in the refrigerator for best results.
- Heat vegetable oil in a large pot or Dutch oven over medium-high heat.
- Add the marinated goat meat and brown on all sides. Remove the meat and set aside.
- In the same pot, add the chopped onion, garlic, and grated ginger. Cook until the onion is softened and translucent, about 5 minutes.
- Stir in the Scotch bonnet peppers and chopped tomato. Cook for another 2 minutes.
- Add the tomato paste, broth, soy sauce, and brown sugar. Stir well to combine.
- Return the goat meat to the pot and bring to a boil.
- Reduce heat to low, cover, and simmer for 1.5 to 2 hours, or until the goat meat is tender and the sauce has thickened. Stir occasionally. Adjust seasoning with salt, black pepper, and lime juice to taste.

2. **Prepare the Wraps:**
   - While the curry goat is cooking, prepare the vegetables for the wraps.
   - Warm the tortillas or flatbreads in a dry skillet or oven.
3. **Assemble the Wraps:**
   - Spread a thin layer of sour cream or Greek yogurt (if using) in the center of each tortilla.
   - Spoon a generous amount of the curry goat mixture onto the tortilla.
   - Top with shredded lettuce or cabbage, diced tomatoes, sliced red onion, sliced cucumber, and chopped fresh cilantro.
   - Squeeze a little lime juice over the top if desired.
4. **Serve:**
   - Roll up the tortillas tightly and cut in half if desired.
   - Serve immediately with extra lime wedges on the side.

Enjoy your Curry Goat Wraps, a flavorful and satisfying meal with a perfect balance of spicy, savory, and fresh ingredients!

Sweet and Sour Shrimp Stir-Fry

Ingredients:

For the Shrimp:

- 1 lb (450g) large shrimp, peeled and deveined
- 1 tablespoon cornstarch
- 1 tablespoon vegetable oil (for cooking)

For the Sweet and Sour Sauce:

- 1/4 cup rice vinegar or white vinegar
- 1/4 cup soy sauce (or tamari for gluten-free)
- 1/4 cup ketchup
- 1/4 cup brown sugar
- 1 tablespoon honey or maple syrup
- 1 tablespoon soy sauce
- 1 teaspoon grated fresh ginger
- 1 clove garlic, minced
- 1 teaspoon cornstarch mixed with 2 tablespoons water (for thickening)

For the Stir-Fry:

- 2 tablespoons vegetable oil (for stir-frying)
- 1 red bell pepper, sliced
- 1 green bell pepper, sliced
- 1 cup broccoli florets
- 1/2 cup sliced carrots
- 1/2 cup snap peas or snow peas
- 1 small onion, sliced
- 2 green onions, sliced (for garnish)
- Sesame seeds (for garnish, optional)

For Serving:

- Cooked jasmine rice or steamed rice

Instructions:

1. **Prepare the Shrimp:**
   - Toss the shrimp with 1 tablespoon of cornstarch until evenly coated.
   - Heat 1 tablespoon of vegetable oil in a large skillet or wok over medium-high heat.
   - Add the shrimp and cook for 2-3 minutes per side, or until pink and opaque. Remove the shrimp from the skillet and set aside.
2. **Make the Sweet and Sour Sauce:**

- In a medium bowl, whisk together rice vinegar, soy sauce, ketchup, brown sugar, honey, soy sauce, grated ginger, and minced garlic.
- Mix the 1 teaspoon cornstarch with 2 tablespoons water and add it to the sauce mixture. Stir well.

3. **Cook the Vegetables:**
   - In the same skillet or wok, add 2 tablespoons of vegetable oil.
   - Stir-fry the sliced onion, bell peppers, broccoli, carrots, and snap peas over medium-high heat for 4-5 minutes, or until the vegetables are crisp-tender.

4. **Combine Ingredients:**
   - Return the cooked shrimp to the skillet with the vegetables.
   - Pour the sweet and sour sauce over the shrimp and vegetables. Stir well to coat everything evenly.
   - Continue to cook for another 2-3 minutes, or until the sauce has thickened and the shrimp and vegetables are heated through.

5. **Serve:**
   - Serve the Sweet and Sour Shrimp Stir-Fry over cooked jasmine rice or steamed rice.
   - Garnish with sliced green onions and sesame seeds if desired.

Enjoy your Sweet and Sour Shrimp Stir-Fry, a flavorful and vibrant dish that's perfect for a quick and satisfying meal!

Caribbean Bean Salad

Ingredients:

For the Salad:

- 1 can (15 oz) black beans, drained and rinsed
- 1 can (15 oz) kidney beans, drained and rinsed
- 1 cup corn kernels (fresh, frozen, or canned)
- 1 cup diced red bell pepper
- 1/2 cup diced red onion
- 1 cup diced mango (fresh or frozen, thawed)
- 1/2 cup chopped fresh cilantro
- 1/4 cup chopped fresh parsley (optional)

For the Dressing:

- 1/4 cup fresh lime juice (about 2 limes)
- 2 tablespoons olive oil
- 1 tablespoon honey or agave syrup
- 1 tablespoon apple cider vinegar
- 1 teaspoon ground cumin
- 1/2 teaspoon smoked paprika
- 1/2 teaspoon garlic powder
- Salt and black pepper, to taste

Instructions:

1. **Prepare the Salad Ingredients:**
   - In a large bowl, combine the black beans, kidney beans, corn kernels, diced red bell pepper, diced red onion, diced mango, and chopped cilantro. (Add parsley if using.)
2. **Make the Dressing:**
   - In a small bowl or jar, whisk together the lime juice, olive oil, honey, apple cider vinegar, ground cumin, smoked paprika, garlic powder, salt, and black pepper.
3. **Combine and Toss:**
   - Pour the dressing over the bean and vegetable mixture.
   - Gently toss everything together until the salad is evenly coated with the dressing.
4. **Chill and Serve:**
   - For best flavor, cover and refrigerate the salad for at least 30 minutes to allow the flavors to meld.
   - Serve chilled or at room temperature.

Enjoy your Caribbean Bean Salad, a vibrant and nutritious dish that's perfect for picnics, barbecues, or as a refreshing side to any meal!

Coconut-Crusted Fish Tacos

Ingredients:

For the Coconut-Crusted Fish:

- 1 lb (450g) white fish fillets (such as cod, tilapia, or snapper)
- 1 cup shredded coconut (sweetened or unsweetened, as preferred)
- 1/2 cup panko breadcrumbs
- 1/4 cup all-purpose flour
- 2 large eggs, beaten
- 1 teaspoon paprika
- 1/2 teaspoon garlic powder
- 1/2 teaspoon onion powder
- Salt and black pepper, to taste
- Vegetable oil (for frying)

For the Slaw:

- 2 cups shredded cabbage (green or red, or a mix)
- 1 cup shredded carrots
- 1/4 cup chopped fresh cilantro
- 1/4 cup mayonnaise
- 2 tablespoons lime juice (about 1 lime)
- 1 tablespoon honey
- Salt and black pepper, to taste

For Assembly:

- 8 small corn or flour tortillas
- Lime wedges (for serving)
- Extra chopped cilantro (for garnish)

Instructions:

1. **Prepare the Fish:**
    - Preheat the oven to 400°F (200°C) if baking. Otherwise, prepare a skillet for frying.
    - Set up a breading station: In one bowl, place the flour. In another bowl, place the beaten eggs. In a third bowl, mix the shredded coconut, panko breadcrumbs, paprika, garlic powder, onion powder, salt, and black pepper.
    - Dip each fish fillet into the flour, shaking off excess, then into the beaten eggs, and finally into the coconut mixture, pressing gently to adhere.
2. **Cook the Fish:**

- **For Frying:** Heat 2-3 tablespoons of vegetable oil in a large skillet over medium heat. Fry the fish fillets for 3-4 minutes per side, or until golden brown and cooked through. Remove and drain on paper towels.
- **For Baking:** Place the breaded fish fillets on a baking sheet lined with parchment paper. Lightly spray or brush with oil. Bake for 15-20 minutes, or until golden brown and cooked through, flipping halfway through.

3. **Prepare the Slaw:**
   - In a large bowl, combine shredded cabbage, shredded carrots, and chopped cilantro.
   - In a small bowl, whisk together mayonnaise, lime juice, honey, salt, and black pepper.
   - Pour the dressing over the slaw and toss to combine.

4. **Assemble the Tacos:**
   - Warm the tortillas in a dry skillet or oven.
   - Slice the cooked fish into strips or chunks.
   - Place a few pieces of fish on each tortilla.
   - Top with a generous amount of the slaw.
   - Garnish with extra chopped cilantro and lime wedges.

5. **Serve:**
   - Serve the Coconut-Crusted Fish Tacos immediately, with lime wedges on the side for extra zest.

Enjoy your Coconut-Crusted Fish Tacos, a perfect blend of crispy, tropical flavors with a refreshing slaw!

Roasted Plantain and Avocado Salad

Ingredients:

For the Salad:

- 2 ripe plantains, peeled and sliced into 1/2-inch rounds
- 1 tablespoon olive oil (for roasting)
- Salt and black pepper, to taste
- 2 ripe avocados, diced
- 1 cup cherry tomatoes, halved
- 1/2 small red onion, thinly sliced
- 1/4 cup chopped fresh cilantro
- 1/4 cup crumbled feta cheese or goat cheese (optional)

For the Dressing:

- 3 tablespoons olive oil
- 2 tablespoons lime juice (about 1 lime)
- 1 tablespoon honey or maple syrup
- 1 teaspoon Dijon mustard
- 1 clove garlic, minced
- Salt and black pepper, to taste

Instructions:

1. **Roast the Plantains:**
   - Preheat your oven to 425°F (220°C).
   - Line a baking sheet with parchment paper or lightly grease it.
   - Toss the plantain slices with olive oil, salt, and black pepper.
   - Spread the plantain slices in a single layer on the baking sheet.
   - Roast for 20-25 minutes, flipping halfway through, until the plantains are golden brown and caramelized. Allow to cool slightly.
2. **Prepare the Salad Ingredients:**
   - In a large bowl, combine the diced avocados, cherry tomatoes, sliced red onion, and chopped cilantro.
   - Add the roasted plantains to the bowl once they have cooled slightly.
3. **Make the Dressing:**
   - In a small bowl or jar, whisk together olive oil, lime juice, honey, Dijon mustard, minced garlic, salt, and black pepper until well combined.
4. **Combine and Serve:**
   - Drizzle the dressing over the salad and gently toss to coat all the ingredients evenly.
   - Sprinkle crumbled feta or goat cheese on top if using.

- Serve immediately, or chill for up to 30 minutes before serving.

Enjoy your Roasted Plantain and Avocado Salad, a delightful mix of sweet, creamy, and fresh flavors with a zesty dressing!

Island-Style BBQ Ribs

Ingredients:

For the Ribs:

- 2 racks of baby back ribs (about 3-4 lbs or 1.4-1.8 kg total)
- 1 tablespoon olive oil
- Salt and black pepper, to taste

For the Marinade:

- 1/4 cup soy sauce (or tamari for gluten-free)
- 1/4 cup fresh lime juice (about 2 limes)
- 1/4 cup brown sugar
- 2 tablespoons honey
- 2 tablespoons grated fresh ginger
- 3 cloves garlic, minced
- 1-2 teaspoons jerk seasoning (adjust to taste)
- 1 teaspoon ground allspice
- 1/2 teaspoon ground cumin
- 1/2 teaspoon ground cinnamon
- 1/4 teaspoon cayenne pepper (optional, for extra heat)

For the BBQ Sauce:

- 1 cup ketchup
- 1/4 cup pineapple juice
- 1/4 cup brown sugar
- 2 tablespoons soy sauce (or tamari for gluten-free)
- 2 tablespoons apple cider vinegar
- 1 tablespoon honey
- 1 teaspoon smoked paprika
- 1/2 teaspoon garlic powder
- 1/2 teaspoon onion powder
- 1/4 teaspoon ground black pepper

Instructions:

1. **Prepare the Ribs:**
   - Remove the membrane from the back of the ribs if it hasn't already been removed. This helps make the ribs more tender.
   - Rub the ribs with olive oil and season with salt and black pepper.
   - Place the ribs in a large resealable plastic bag or shallow dish.

2. **Marinate the Ribs:**
    - In a bowl, whisk together soy sauce, lime juice, brown sugar, honey, grated ginger, minced garlic, jerk seasoning, ground allspice, ground cumin, ground cinnamon, and cayenne pepper (if using).
    - Pour the marinade over the ribs, ensuring they are well coated.
    - Seal the bag or cover the dish and refrigerate for at least 2 hours, or overnight for best results.
3. **Prepare the BBQ Sauce:**
    - In a medium saucepan, combine ketchup, pineapple juice, brown sugar, soy sauce, apple cider vinegar, honey, smoked paprika, garlic powder, onion powder, and ground black pepper.
    - Bring to a simmer over medium heat, stirring occasionally.
    - Reduce heat and simmer for 10-15 minutes, or until the sauce has thickened slightly. Remove from heat and let it cool.
4. **Cook the Ribs:**
    - Preheat your grill to medium heat or your oven to 300°F (150°C).
    - If using a grill, prepare it for indirect grilling by heating one side of the grill and leaving the other side cooler. If using the oven, line a baking sheet with foil.
    - Remove the ribs from the marinade and discard the marinade.
    - If grilling, place the ribs on the cooler side of the grill and cook with the lid closed for about 1.5 to 2 hours, or until tender, basting occasionally with BBQ sauce.
    - If baking, place the ribs on the prepared baking sheet and bake for 2.5 to 3 hours, or until tender. Brush with BBQ sauce during the last 30 minutes of baking.
5. **Finish and Serve:**
    - If grilling, you can finish the ribs over direct heat for a few minutes per side to caramelize the BBQ sauce.
    - Let the ribs rest for a few minutes before cutting into individual portions.
    - Serve with extra BBQ sauce on the side and your favorite sides.

Enjoy your Island-Style BBQ Ribs, with their tender, juicy meat and sweet, tangy tropical flavors!

Spiced Sweet Potato and Black Bean Burritos

Ingredients:

For the Filling:

- 2 medium sweet potatoes, peeled and diced into 1/2-inch cubes
- 1 tablespoon olive oil
- 1 teaspoon ground cumin
- 1 teaspoon smoked paprika
- 1/2 teaspoon chili powder
- 1/2 teaspoon garlic powder
- 1/2 teaspoon onion powder
- 1/4 teaspoon cayenne pepper (optional, for extra heat)
- Salt and black pepper, to taste
- 1 can (15 oz) black beans, drained and rinsed
- 1 cup corn kernels (fresh, frozen, or canned)
- 1 cup diced red bell pepper
- 1/2 cup diced red onion
- 1/2 cup chopped fresh cilantro

For the Burritos:

- 4 large flour tortillas (or whole wheat for a healthier option)
- 1 cup shredded cheddar cheese or Monterey Jack cheese (optional)
- 1/2 cup sour cream or Greek yogurt (optional)
- 1/2 cup salsa or pico de gallo (optional)

Instructions:

1. **Prepare the Sweet Potatoes:**
   - Preheat your oven to 400°F (200°C).
   - Toss the diced sweet potatoes with olive oil, ground cumin, smoked paprika, chili powder, garlic powder, onion powder, cayenne pepper (if using), salt, and black pepper.
   - Spread the sweet potatoes in a single layer on a baking sheet.
   - Roast for 25-30 minutes, or until the sweet potatoes are tender and lightly caramelized. Stir halfway through cooking.
2. **Prepare the Filling:**
   - In a large bowl, combine the roasted sweet potatoes, black beans, corn, diced red bell pepper, diced red onion, and chopped fresh cilantro. Mix well.
3. **Assemble the Burritos:**
   - Warm the tortillas in a dry skillet or microwave until pliable.
   - If using cheese, sprinkle a small amount of shredded cheese in the center of each tortilla.

        - Spoon the sweet potato and black bean mixture onto each tortilla.
        - Top with additional cheese if desired.
        - Fold in the sides of the tortilla and roll it up from the bottom to form a tight wrap.
4. **Optional – Heat the Burritos:**
        - For a crispier wrap, heat a skillet over medium heat.
        - Place the burritos seam-side down and cook for 2-3 minutes per side, or until golden brown and crispy.
5. **Serve:**
        - Slice the burritos in half if desired.
        - Serve with sour cream or Greek yogurt, salsa or pico de gallo, and extra chopped cilantro if desired.

Enjoy your Spiced Sweet Potato and Black Bean Burritos, a flavorful and filling meal that's perfect for lunch or dinner!

Mango and Chicken Lettuce Wraps

Ingredients:

For the Chicken Filling:

- 1 lb (450g) boneless, skinless chicken breasts or thighs, diced
- 2 tablespoons olive oil or vegetable oil
- 1 small onion, finely chopped
- 2 cloves garlic, minced
- 1 red bell pepper, diced
- 1 cup fresh mango, diced
- 2 tablespoons soy sauce (or tamari for gluten-free)
- 1 tablespoon hoisin sauce
- 1 tablespoon rice vinegar
- 1 teaspoon grated fresh ginger
- 1/2 teaspoon ground cumin
- 1/2 teaspoon smoked paprika
- 1/4 teaspoon crushed red pepper flakes (optional, for heat)
- Salt and black pepper, to taste

For the Lettuce Wraps:

- 1 head of butter lettuce or iceberg lettuce (about 8-10 large leaves)
- 1/4 cup chopped fresh cilantro
- 1/4 cup sliced green onions
- Lime wedges (for serving)
- Optional: chopped peanuts or cashews (for garnish)

Instructions:

1. **Prepare the Chicken Filling:**
   - Heat the oil in a large skillet over medium-high heat.
   - Add the diced chicken and cook until browned and cooked through, about 5-7 minutes. Remove the chicken from the skillet and set aside.
   - In the same skillet, add the chopped onion and cook until softened, about 3 minutes.
   - Add the minced garlic and diced red bell pepper. Cook for another 2 minutes until the pepper is tender.
   - Return the chicken to the skillet.
   - Stir in the diced mango, soy sauce, hoisin sauce, rice vinegar, grated ginger, ground cumin, smoked paprika, and crushed red pepper flakes (if using).
   - Cook for 2-3 minutes, or until the mango is heated through and the sauce has slightly thickened. Season with salt and black pepper to taste.
2. **Assemble the Lettuce Wraps:**

- - Gently separate the lettuce leaves and wash them thoroughly. Pat dry with a paper towel.
  - Spoon a generous amount of the chicken and mango mixture into the center of each lettuce leaf.
  - Top with chopped fresh cilantro and sliced green onions.
  - Garnish with chopped peanuts or cashews if desired.
3. **Serve:**
    - Serve the Mango and Chicken Lettuce Wraps with lime wedges on the side for a fresh squeeze of lime juice.

Enjoy your Mango and Chicken Lettuce Wraps, a refreshing and tasty dish with a perfect balance of sweet, savory, and tangy flavors!

Spicy Caribbean Meatballs

Ingredients:

For the Meatballs:

- 1 lb (450g) ground beef or ground chicken
- 1/2 cup bread crumbs (plain or seasoned)
- 1/4 cup finely chopped onion
- 2 cloves garlic, minced
- 1/4 cup finely chopped fresh cilantro
- 1 egg
- 1 teaspoon ground allspice
- 1 teaspoon paprika
- 1/2 teaspoon ground cumin
- 1/2 teaspoon dried thyme
- 1/4 teaspoon cayenne pepper (adjust to taste for spiciness)
- 1/2 teaspoon salt
- 1/4 teaspoon black pepper
- 1 tablespoon soy sauce (or tamari for gluten-free)
- 1 tablespoon vegetable oil (for cooking)

For the Spicy Caribbean Sauce:

- 1 cup tomato sauce
- 1/4 cup pineapple juice
- 2 tablespoons soy sauce (or tamari for gluten-free)
- 2 tablespoons brown sugar
- 1 tablespoon apple cider vinegar
- 1 teaspoon grated fresh ginger
- 1-2 teaspoons Scotch bonnet pepper sauce (or other hot sauce, adjust to taste)
- 1/2 teaspoon ground allspice
- 1/4 teaspoon ground cinnamon
- Salt and black pepper, to taste

Instructions:

1. **Prepare the Meatballs:**
    - Preheat your oven to 375°F (190°C).
    - In a large bowl, combine ground beef or chicken, bread crumbs, finely chopped onion, minced garlic, chopped cilantro, egg, ground allspice, paprika, ground cumin, dried thyme, cayenne pepper, salt, black pepper, and soy sauce.
    - Mix until just combined; avoid overmixing to keep the meatballs tender.
    - Form the mixture into 1-inch meatballs and place them on a baking sheet lined with parchment paper.

2. **Cook the Meatballs:**
    - Heat 1 tablespoon of vegetable oil in a large skillet over medium heat.
    - Brown the meatballs on all sides in batches if necessary, about 5-7 minutes. They do not need to be fully cooked through at this stage.
    - Transfer the browned meatballs to a baking sheet and finish cooking in the preheated oven for 10-12 minutes, or until cooked through.
3. **Make the Spicy Caribbean Sauce:**
    - In a medium saucepan, combine tomato sauce, pineapple juice, soy sauce, brown sugar, apple cider vinegar, grated ginger, Scotch bonnet pepper sauce, ground allspice, and ground cinnamon.
    - Bring to a simmer over medium heat, stirring occasionally.
    - Reduce heat and simmer for 10 minutes, or until the sauce has thickened slightly. Season with salt and black pepper to taste.
4. **Combine and Serve:**
    - Toss the cooked meatballs in the spicy Caribbean sauce until well coated.
    - Serve the meatballs with additional sauce on the side, if desired.

Enjoy your Spicy Caribbean Meatballs, a perfect blend of spicy, sweet, and savory flavors that are sure to impress!

Coconut Milk Chicken Soup

Ingredients:

For the Soup:

- 1 lb (450g) boneless, skinless chicken breasts or thighs, diced
- 1 tablespoon olive oil or vegetable oil
- 1 medium onion, finely chopped
- 3 cloves garlic, minced
- 1 tablespoon fresh ginger, minced
- 1 red bell pepper, diced
- 2 carrots, sliced
- 1 cup mushrooms, sliced (optional)
- 1 can (14 oz) coconut milk (full-fat or light)
- 4 cups chicken broth or vegetable broth
- 2 tablespoons fish sauce or soy sauce
- 1 tablespoon lime juice (about 1 lime)
- 1 tablespoon curry powder
- 1/2 teaspoon ground turmeric
- 1/4 teaspoon crushed red pepper flakes (optional, for heat)
- Salt and black pepper, to taste
- 1 cup baby spinach or kale (optional)
- 1/4 cup fresh cilantro, chopped (for garnish)
- Lime wedges (for serving)

Instructions:

1. **Cook the Chicken:**
   - Heat the oil in a large pot over medium heat.
   - Add the diced chicken and cook until browned and cooked through, about 5-7 minutes. Remove the chicken from the pot and set aside.
2. **Prepare the Soup Base:**
   - In the same pot, add the chopped onion and cook until softened and translucent, about 3 minutes.
   - Add the minced garlic and ginger, and cook for another 1 minute until fragrant.
   - Stir in the diced red bell pepper, sliced carrots, and mushrooms (if using). Cook for 5 minutes, or until the vegetables start to soften.
3. **Add the Liquid Ingredients:**
   - Pour in the coconut milk and chicken broth, stirring to combine.
   - Add the fish sauce (or soy sauce), lime juice, curry powder, ground turmeric, and crushed red pepper flakes (if using).
   - Bring the soup to a gentle simmer and cook for 10 minutes, or until the vegetables are tender.
4. **Finish the Soup:**

- Return the cooked chicken to the pot and stir well.
- Add the baby spinach or kale, if using, and cook for an additional 2-3 minutes until wilted and heated through.
- Season with salt and black pepper to taste.
5. **Serve:**
   - Ladle the soup into bowls.
   - Garnish with chopped fresh cilantro.
   - Serve with lime wedges on the side for an extra burst of freshness.

Enjoy your Coconut Milk Chicken Soup, a rich and comforting dish with tropical flavors that's perfect for a cozy meal!

Jamaican Beef and Cheese Patties

Ingredients:

For the Pastry:

- 2 1/2 cups all-purpose flour
- 1/2 teaspoon salt
- 1 teaspoon paprika
- 1/2 teaspoon turmeric (for color)
- 1/2 cup cold unsalted butter, cut into small cubes
- 1/4 cup cold shortening or lard (optional, for extra flakiness)
- 1 large egg
- 1/4 cup cold water (or as needed)

For the Beef Filling:

- 1 lb (450g) ground beef
- 1 tablespoon vegetable oil
- 1 small onion, finely chopped
- 2 cloves garlic, minced
- 1 small green bell pepper, finely chopped
- 1 small red bell pepper, finely chopped
- 1 teaspoon ground allspice
- 1/2 teaspoon ground thyme
- 1 teaspoon paprika
- 1/2 teaspoon curry powder
- 1/4 teaspoon cayenne pepper (optional, for heat)
- 1/2 cup beef broth or water
- 1 tablespoon soy sauce
- Salt and black pepper, to taste
- 1/2 cup shredded cheddar cheese (or your choice of cheese)
- 1 tablespoon tomato paste (optional)

For Assembly:

- 1 large egg, beaten (for egg wash)

Instructions:

1. **Make the Pastry:**
   - In a large bowl, combine flour, salt, paprika, and turmeric.
   - Cut in the cold butter and shortening (if using) with a pastry cutter or your fingers until the mixture resembles coarse crumbs.
   - In a small bowl, whisk together the egg and cold water.
   - Gradually add the egg mixture to the flour mixture, stirring until the dough begins to come together. You may need to add a bit more water if the dough is too dry.
   - Turn the dough out onto a lightly floured surface and knead briefly until smooth.

- Divide the dough into 8-10 equal portions and flatten into discs. Wrap each disc in plastic wrap and refrigerate for at least 30 minutes.
2. **Prepare the Beef Filling:**
    - Heat the vegetable oil in a large skillet over medium heat.
    - Add the ground beef and cook, breaking it up with a spoon, until browned and cooked through.
    - Add the chopped onion, garlic, green bell pepper, and red bell pepper. Cook for 3-4 minutes until the vegetables are softened.
    - Stir in ground allspice, ground thyme, paprika, curry powder, cayenne pepper (if using), and tomato paste (if using). Cook for 1-2 minutes until fragrant.
    - Pour in the beef broth or water and soy sauce. Simmer for 5-7 minutes, or until the mixture is thickened. Season with salt and black pepper to taste.
    - Remove from heat and let cool slightly. Stir in shredded cheese until melted and well combined.
3. **Assemble the Patties:**
    - Preheat your oven to 375°F (190°C). Line a baking sheet with parchment paper.
    - Roll out each dough disc on a lightly floured surface into a 6-8 inch circle.
    - Place a generous spoonful of the beef filling in the center of each circle.
    - Fold the dough over to create a half-moon shape, sealing the edges by pressing with a fork or crimping with your fingers.
    - Brush the tops of the patties with the beaten egg for a golden finish.
4. **Bake the Patties:**
    - Place the patties on the prepared baking sheet.
    - Bake for 25-30 minutes, or until the pastry is golden brown and crisp.
5. **Serve:**
    - Let the patties cool slightly before serving.

Enjoy your Jamaican Beef and Cheese Patties, a delicious and satisfying treat with a perfect combination of spicy beef and gooey cheese in a flaky pastry shell!

Pineapple Salsa Chicken Enchiladas

Ingredients:

For the Chicken Filling:

- 1 lb (450g) boneless, skinless chicken breasts or thighs
- 1 tablespoon olive oil
- 1 teaspoon ground cumin
- 1 teaspoon paprika
- 1/2 teaspoon garlic powder
- 1/2 teaspoon onion powder
- 1/4 teaspoon cayenne pepper (optional, for heat)
- Salt and black pepper, to taste
- 1 cup pineapple salsa (store-bought or homemade)
- 1/2 cup shredded cheddar cheese (or Monterey Jack, or your favorite cheese)
- 1/4 cup chopped fresh cilantro

For the Enchiladas:

- 8 small flour or corn tortillas
- 2 cups enchilada sauce (store-bought or homemade)
- 1 cup shredded cheddar cheese (or Monterey Jack, or your favorite cheese)
- 1/4 cup chopped fresh cilantro (for garnish)

For Homemade Pineapple Salsa (if making your own):

- 1 cup fresh pineapple, finely diced
- 1/2 cup diced red bell pepper
- 1/4 cup finely chopped red onion
- 1 small jalapeño, seeded and minced (optional, for heat)
- 2 tablespoons fresh lime juice
- 1 tablespoon chopped fresh cilantro
- Salt to taste

Instructions:

1. **Prepare the Chicken Filling:**
   - Preheat your oven to 375°F (190°C).
   - Season the chicken breasts or thighs with ground cumin, paprika, garlic powder, onion powder, cayenne pepper (if using), salt, and black pepper.
   - Heat olive oil in a large skillet over medium heat. Cook the chicken for 6-7 minutes per side, or until cooked through and golden brown. The internal temperature should reach 165°F (74°C).
   - Remove the chicken from the skillet and let it rest for a few minutes before shredding it with two forks.

- In the same skillet, add the shredded chicken and pineapple salsa. Stir to combine and heat through. Remove from heat and mix in 1/2 cup shredded cheese and chopped cilantro.
2. **Prepare the Pineapple Salsa (if making your own):**
    - In a medium bowl, combine finely diced pineapple, red bell pepper, red onion, jalapeño (if using), lime juice, chopped cilantro, and salt. Mix well and set aside.
3. **Assemble the Enchiladas:**
    - Lightly grease a 9x13-inch baking dish.
    - Pour 1/2 cup of enchilada sauce into the bottom of the baking dish and spread it out.
    - Place a spoonful of the chicken mixture in the center of each tortilla, then roll up the tortilla and place it seam-side down in the baking dish. Repeat with the remaining tortillas.
    - Pour the remaining enchilada sauce over the rolled tortillas, spreading it evenly.
    - Sprinkle the top with 1 cup of shredded cheese.
4. **Bake the Enchiladas:**
    - Bake for 20-25 minutes, or until the cheese is melted and bubbly, and the enchiladas are heated through.
5. **Serve:**
    - Garnish with additional chopped fresh cilantro.
    - Serve with a side of the homemade pineapple salsa (or store-bought) for extra flavor and freshness.

Enjoy your Pineapple Salsa Chicken Enchiladas, a delightful fusion of sweet, savory, and tangy flavors in a comforting and satisfying dish!

Tropical Pork and Pineapple Skewers

Ingredients:

For the Marinade:

- 1/4 cup soy sauce (or tamari for gluten-free)
- 1/4 cup pineapple juice
- 2 tablespoons brown sugar
- 2 tablespoons rice vinegar
- 1 tablespoon grated fresh ginger
- 2 cloves garlic, minced
- 1 tablespoon vegetable oil
- 1 teaspoon ground allspice
- 1/2 teaspoon ground cumin
- 1/4 teaspoon cayenne pepper (optional, for heat)
- Salt and black pepper, to taste

For the Skewers:

- 1 lb (450g) pork tenderloin or pork loin, cut into 1-inch cubes
- 1 cup fresh pineapple, cut into 1-inch chunks
- 1 red bell pepper, cut into 1-inch chunks
- 1 yellow bell pepper, cut into 1-inch chunks
- 1 small red onion, cut into wedges
- Wooden or metal skewers (if using wooden skewers, soak them in water for 30 minutes before grilling)

Instructions:

1. **Prepare the Marinade:**
    - In a medium bowl, whisk together soy sauce, pineapple juice, brown sugar, rice vinegar, grated ginger, minced garlic, vegetable oil, ground allspice, ground cumin, cayenne pepper (if using), salt, and black pepper.
2. **Marinate the Pork:**
    - Place the pork cubes in a resealable plastic bag or shallow dish.
    - Pour the marinade over the pork, ensuring all pieces are well coated.
    - Seal the bag or cover the dish and refrigerate for at least 1 hour, or overnight for best results.
3. **Assemble the Skewers:**
    - Preheat your grill to medium-high heat.
    - Thread the marinated pork cubes, pineapple chunks, red bell pepper, yellow bell pepper, and red onion onto the skewers, alternating ingredients as you go.
4. **Grill the Skewers:**
    - Lightly oil the grill grates to prevent sticking.

- Place the skewers on the grill and cook, turning occasionally, for about 10-12 minutes, or until the pork is cooked through and has reached an internal temperature of 145°F (63°C) and the vegetables are tender and slightly charred.

5. **Serve:**
    - Remove the skewers from the grill and let them rest for a few minutes.
    - Serve the Tropical Pork and Pineapple Skewers hot, garnished with fresh cilantro or parsley if desired.

Enjoy your Tropical Pork and Pineapple Skewers, a delicious and visually appealing dish with a perfect balance of sweet, savory, and smoky flavors!

Coconut and Lime Seafood Pasta

Ingredients:

For the Pasta:

- 12 oz (340g) pasta (such as linguine, fettuccine, or spaghetti)
- Salt, for the pasta water

For the Seafood:

- 1 tablespoon olive oil
- 1/2 lb (225g) shrimp, peeled and deveined
- 1/2 lb (225g) scallops (or your choice of seafood)
- 1/2 teaspoon paprika
- 1/2 teaspoon garlic powder
- Salt and black pepper, to taste

For the Sauce:

- 1 tablespoon olive oil
- 1 small onion, finely chopped
- 3 cloves garlic, minced
- 1 can (14 oz) coconut milk
- 1/2 cup chicken broth or seafood broth
- 1 tablespoon lime juice (about 1 lime)
- 1 teaspoon lime zest
- 1 teaspoon grated fresh ginger
- 1 teaspoon soy sauce (or tamari for gluten-free)
- 1/4 teaspoon crushed red pepper flakes (optional, for heat)
- 1 tablespoon chopped fresh cilantro (for garnish)

Instructions:

1. **Cook the Pasta:**
    - Bring a large pot of salted water to a boil.
    - Cook the pasta according to the package instructions until al dente. Drain and set aside.
2. **Prepare the Seafood:**
    - In a large skillet, heat 1 tablespoon of olive oil over medium-high heat.
    - Season the shrimp and scallops with paprika, garlic powder, salt, and black pepper.
    - Add the shrimp and scallops to the skillet and cook for 2-3 minutes per side, or until the shrimp are pink and opaque and the scallops are cooked through and slightly golden. Remove the seafood from the skillet and set aside.
3. **Make the Sauce:**

- In the same skillet, add 1 tablespoon of olive oil.
- Sauté the chopped onion over medium heat until softened and translucent, about 3-4 minutes.
- Add the minced garlic and cook for an additional 1 minute until fragrant.
- Pour in the coconut milk and chicken broth, stirring to combine.
- Bring to a simmer and cook for 5 minutes, allowing the sauce to reduce slightly.
- Stir in the lime juice, lime zest, grated ginger, soy sauce, and crushed red pepper flakes (if using). Cook for an additional 2 minutes.
- Season with salt and black pepper to taste.

4. **Combine Pasta and Seafood:**
    - Add the cooked pasta to the sauce and toss to coat.
    - Gently fold in the cooked seafood and heat through, about 2 minutes.
5. **Serve:**
    - Divide the pasta and seafood among serving plates.
    - Garnish with chopped fresh cilantro.

Enjoy your Coconut and Lime Seafood Pasta, a creamy and zesty dish with a perfect blend of tropical flavors and tender seafood!

Grilled Chicken and Pineapple Salad

Ingredients:

For the Salad:

- 2 boneless, skinless chicken breasts
- 1 tablespoon olive oil
- 1 teaspoon ground cumin
- 1 teaspoon paprika
- 1/2 teaspoon garlic powder
- 1/2 teaspoon onion powder
- Salt and black pepper, to taste
- 1 cup fresh pineapple, diced (about 1/2 of a small pineapple or 1 cup of pre-cut pineapple)
- 4 cups mixed salad greens (such as romaine, spinach, and arugula)
- 1 cup cherry tomatoes, halved
- 1/2 cucumber, sliced
- 1/4 red onion, thinly sliced
- 1/4 cup sliced almonds or chopped nuts (optional)
- 1/4 cup crumbled feta cheese or goat cheese (optional)

For the Dressing:

- 3 tablespoons olive oil
- 2 tablespoons pineapple juice
- 1 tablespoon honey
- 1 tablespoon apple cider vinegar
- 1 teaspoon Dijon mustard
- 1 teaspoon grated fresh ginger
- Salt and black pepper, to taste

Instructions:

1. **Prepare the Chicken:**
   - Preheat your grill to medium-high heat.
   - Rub the chicken breasts with olive oil, ground cumin, paprika, garlic powder, onion powder, salt, and black pepper.
   - Grill the chicken for 6-8 minutes per side, or until fully cooked and the internal temperature reaches 165°F (74°C). Remove from the grill and let rest for 5 minutes before slicing.
2. **Prepare the Dressing:**
   - In a small bowl, whisk together olive oil, pineapple juice, honey, apple cider vinegar, Dijon mustard, grated ginger, salt, and black pepper until well combined.
3. **Assemble the Salad:**
   - In a large salad bowl, combine mixed salad greens, cherry tomatoes, cucumber, and red onion.

        - Dice the grilled chicken and add it to the salad along with the diced pineapple.
        - If using, sprinkle the salad with sliced almonds or chopped nuts and crumbled feta or goat cheese.
4. **Dress and Serve:**
        - Drizzle the dressing over the salad and toss gently to combine.
        - Serve immediately or chill until ready to serve.

Enjoy your Grilled Chicken and Pineapple Salad, a vibrant and satisfying meal with a delightful mix of flavors and textures!

Jerk Tempeh Wraps

Ingredients:

For the Jerk Tempeh:

- 1 package (8 oz) tempeh, sliced into thin strips
- 2 tablespoons jerk seasoning (store-bought or homemade)
- 1 tablespoon olive oil
- 1 tablespoon soy sauce (or tamari for gluten-free)
- 1 tablespoon lime juice (about 1 lime)

For the Lime Sauce:

- 1/2 cup plain Greek yogurt (or dairy-free yogurt for vegan)
- 1 tablespoon lime juice (about 1 lime)
- 1 teaspoon honey or agave syrup
- 1 teaspoon chopped fresh cilantro (optional)
- Salt and black pepper, to taste

For the Wraps:

- 4 large flour tortillas or whole wheat tortillas
- 1 cup shredded lettuce or mixed greens
- 1 cup cherry tomatoes, halved
- 1/2 cucumber, thinly sliced
- 1/4 red onion, thinly sliced
- 1 avocado, sliced
- Optional: sliced jalapeños for extra heat

Instructions:

1. **Prepare the Jerk Tempeh:**
   - In a bowl, mix the jerk seasoning with olive oil, soy sauce, and lime juice.
   - Add the tempeh strips and toss to coat evenly.
   - Heat a large skillet over medium heat and add a little oil if needed.
   - Add the tempeh strips to the skillet and cook for 5-7 minutes, turning occasionally, until the tempeh is golden brown and crispy on the edges. Remove from heat and set aside.
2. **Prepare the Lime Sauce:**
   - In a small bowl, whisk together Greek yogurt, lime juice, honey or agave syrup, and chopped cilantro (if using).
   - Season with salt and black pepper to taste.
3. **Assemble the Wraps:**
   - Warm the tortillas slightly in a dry skillet or microwave to make them more pliable.
   - Spread a generous amount of the lime sauce over each tortilla.

- Layer shredded lettuce or mixed greens, cherry tomatoes, cucumber, red onion, avocado slices, and the jerk tempeh strips on each tortilla.
 - Add sliced jalapeños if desired.
4. **Wrap and Serve:**
 - Roll up each tortilla tightly, folding in the sides as you go to secure the filling.
 - Slice the wraps in half and serve immediately.

Enjoy your Jerk Tempeh Wraps, a flavorful and satisfying meal with a perfect blend of spicy, tangy, and fresh ingredients!

Caribbean Shrimp and Grits

Ingredients:

For the Shrimp:

- 1 lb (450g) large shrimp, peeled and deveined
- 2 tablespoons olive oil
- 1 tablespoon jerk seasoning (store-bought or homemade)
- 1/2 teaspoon paprika
- 1/2 teaspoon garlic powder
- 1/4 teaspoon cayenne pepper (optional, for extra heat)
- Salt and black pepper, to taste
- 2 cloves garlic, minced
- 1/2 cup diced red bell pepper
- 1/2 cup diced green bell pepper
- 1/4 cup diced red onion
- 1/4 cup chopped fresh cilantro

For the Grits:

- 1 cup grits (stone-ground or quick-cooking)
- 4 cups water or chicken broth
- 1 cup shredded cheddar cheese (or your choice of cheese)
- 2 tablespoons unsalted butter
- Salt and black pepper, to taste

For Garnish:

- Chopped fresh cilantro
- Lime wedges

Instructions:

1. **Prepare the Grits:**
   - In a medium saucepan, bring 4 cups of water or chicken broth to a boil.
   - Gradually stir in the grits, reducing the heat to low.
   - Cook, stirring occasionally, for about 5 minutes if using quick-cooking grits, or according to package instructions if using stone-ground grits (usually about 20-30 minutes), until thickened and tender.
   - Stir in the shredded cheese and butter. Season with salt and black pepper to taste. Keep warm.
2. **Prepare the Shrimp:**
   - In a large bowl, toss the shrimp with jerk seasoning, paprika, garlic powder, cayenne pepper (if using), salt, and black pepper.
   - Heat olive oil in a large skillet over medium-high heat.

- Add the seasoned shrimp and cook for 2-3 minutes per side, or until the shrimp are pink and opaque. Remove the shrimp from the skillet and set aside.
- In the same skillet, add a bit more oil if needed and sauté the minced garlic, diced red and green bell peppers, and diced red onion until softened, about 3-4 minutes.
- Return the shrimp to the skillet and toss to combine with the vegetables. Cook for an additional 1-2 minutes to heat through.
- Stir in the chopped fresh cilantro.

3. **Assemble and Serve:**
    - Spoon a generous portion of creamy grits onto each plate.
    - Top with the Caribbean shrimp and vegetable mixture.
    - Garnish with additional chopped fresh cilantro and lime wedges for squeezing.

Enjoy your Caribbean Shrimp and Grits, a delicious fusion of spicy, creamy, and savory flavors that's sure to be a hit!

Island-style Couscous Salad

Ingredients:

For the Salad:

- 1 cup couscous
- 1 cup boiling water or vegetable broth
- 1 cup diced mango (about 1 ripe mango)
- 1 cup diced pineapple (about 1/2 of a small pineapple or 1 cup of pre-cut pineapple)
- 1/2 cup diced red bell pepper
- 1/2 cup diced cucumber
- 1/4 cup finely chopped red onion
- 1/4 cup chopped fresh cilantro or mint
- 1/4 cup sliced almonds or chopped nuts (optional)

For the Dressing:

- 1/4 cup olive oil
- 2 tablespoons fresh lime juice (about 1 lime)
- 1 tablespoon honey or agave syrup
- 1 teaspoon grated fresh ginger
- 1 teaspoon Dijon mustard
- Salt and black pepper, to taste

Instructions:

1. **Prepare the Couscous:**
    - In a medium bowl, place the couscous.
    - Pour the boiling water or vegetable broth over the couscous.
    - Cover the bowl with a lid or plastic wrap and let it sit for 5 minutes.
    - Fluff the couscous with a fork to separate the grains and let it cool to room temperature.
2. **Prepare the Dressing:**
    - In a small bowl, whisk together olive oil, lime juice, honey or agave syrup, grated ginger, Dijon mustard, salt, and black pepper until well combined.
3. **Assemble the Salad:**
    - In a large bowl, combine the cooled couscous with diced mango, diced pineapple, diced red bell pepper, diced cucumber, red onion, and chopped cilantro or mint.
    - Pour the dressing over the salad and toss gently to combine.
    - If using, sprinkle sliced almonds or chopped nuts on top for added crunch.
4. **Serve:**
    - Chill the salad in the refrigerator for at least 30 minutes before serving to allow the flavors to meld.
    - Serve cold or at room temperature.

Enjoy your Island-Style Couscous Salad, a vibrant and refreshing dish that's perfect as a side or light main course, bursting with tropical flavors and fresh ingredients!

Tropical Chicken Lettuce Cups

Ingredients:

For the Chicken Filling:

- 1 lb (450g) ground chicken
- 1 tablespoon olive oil
- 1 small onion, finely chopped
- 2 cloves garlic, minced
- 1/2 cup diced bell pepper (red, yellow, or green)
- 1/2 cup diced pineapple (fresh or canned)
- 1/4 cup diced water chestnuts (optional, for extra crunch)
- 2 tablespoons soy sauce (or tamari for gluten-free)
- 1 tablespoon hoisin sauce (or use extra soy sauce)
- 1 tablespoon fresh lime juice (about 1 lime)
- 1 teaspoon grated fresh ginger
- 1/2 teaspoon ground cumin
- 1/2 teaspoon paprika
- 1/4 teaspoon crushed red pepper flakes (optional, for heat)
- Salt and black pepper, to taste
- 2 green onions, thinly sliced
- 1/4 cup chopped fresh cilantro

For the Lettuce Cups:

- 1 head of butter lettuce or iceberg lettuce (or a mix), leaves separated and rinsed

For Garnish (optional):

- Extra chopped fresh cilantro
- Lime wedges
- Sliced jalapeños or chopped chili for extra heat

Instructions:

1. **Prepare the Chicken Filling:**
    - Heat olive oil in a large skillet over medium heat.
    - Add the finely chopped onion and cook for 3-4 minutes, until softened.
    - Add the minced garlic and cook for an additional 1 minute, until fragrant.
    - Add the ground chicken to the skillet, breaking it up with a spoon. Cook until browned and fully cooked through, about 5-7 minutes.
    - Stir in the diced bell pepper, pineapple, and water chestnuts (if using). Cook for 2-3 minutes, until the bell pepper is slightly softened.
    - Add the soy sauce, hoisin sauce, lime juice, grated ginger, ground cumin, paprika, and crushed red pepper flakes (if using). Stir to combine and cook for another 2-3 minutes, until the sauce has thickened slightly and the flavors are well combined.

         - Season with salt and black pepper to taste. Stir in the sliced green onions and chopped cilantro.
2. **Assemble the Lettuce Cups:**
         - Arrange the lettuce leaves on a serving platter or individual plates.
         - Spoon the tropical chicken filling into each lettuce leaf.
3. **Garnish and Serve:**
         - Garnish with additional chopped fresh cilantro, lime wedges, and sliced jalapeños or chopped chili if desired.
         - Serve immediately while the filling is warm and the lettuce leaves are crisp.

Enjoy your Tropical Chicken Lettuce Cups, a delightful and fresh dish with a burst of tropical flavors and a satisfying crunch!

Coconut Lime Shrimp Tacos

Ingredients:

For the Shrimp:

- 1 lb (450g) large shrimp, peeled and deveined
- 2 tablespoons coconut oil (or olive oil)
- 1 teaspoon ground cumin
- 1 teaspoon paprika
- 1/2 teaspoon garlic powder
- 1/2 teaspoon onion powder
- 1/2 teaspoon salt
- 1/4 teaspoon black pepper
- 1 tablespoon lime juice (about 1 lime)
- 1 tablespoon chopped fresh cilantro (optional, for garnish)

For the Coconut Lime Sauce:

- 1/2 cup canned coconut milk
- 2 tablespoons lime juice (about 1 lime)
- 1 tablespoon honey or agave syrup
- 1 tablespoon soy sauce (or tamari for gluten-free)
- 1 teaspoon grated fresh ginger
- 1 small garlic clove, minced
- Salt and black pepper, to taste

For the Tacos:

- 8 small tortillas (flour or corn)
- 1 cup shredded cabbage or mixed greens
- 1/2 cup diced mango or pineapple (optional, for added sweetness)
- 1/4 cup chopped red onion
- 1 avocado, sliced
- 1/4 cup chopped fresh cilantro (for garnish)

Instructions:

1. **Prepare the Shrimp:**
    - In a large bowl, toss the shrimp with ground cumin, paprika, garlic powder, onion powder, salt, and black pepper.
    - Heat the coconut oil in a large skillet over medium-high heat.
    - Add the shrimp and cook for 2-3 minutes per side, or until pink and opaque. Drizzle with lime juice during the last minute of cooking.
    - Remove from heat and garnish with chopped fresh cilantro if desired.
2. **Prepare the Coconut Lime Sauce:**
    - In a small bowl, whisk together the coconut milk, lime juice, honey or agave syrup, soy sauce, grated ginger, and minced garlic.
    - Season with salt and black pepper to taste.

3. **Assemble the Tacos:**
    - Warm the tortillas in a dry skillet or microwave to make them more pliable.
    - Spread a spoonful of the coconut lime sauce on each tortilla.
    - Top with shredded cabbage or mixed greens, diced mango or pineapple (if using), chopped red onion, avocado slices, and the cooked shrimp.
4. **Serve:**
    - Garnish with additional chopped fresh cilantro and a squeeze of lime juice if desired.
    - Serve immediately for the best flavor and texture.

Enjoy your Coconut Lime Shrimp Tacos, a flavorful and tropical dish that combines creamy, tangy, and slightly sweet elements for a satisfying meal!

Plantain and Chicken Stew

Ingredients:

For the Stew:

- 1.5 lbs (680g) bone-in, skinless chicken thighs or drumsticks
- 2 tablespoons vegetable oil or olive oil
- 1 large onion, finely chopped
- 3 cloves garlic, minced
- 1 bell pepper (red or green), diced
- 2 large tomatoes, diced (or 1 can of diced tomatoes)
- 1 tablespoon tomato paste
- 1 teaspoon paprika
- 1 teaspoon ground cumin
- 1 teaspoon dried thyme
- 1/2 teaspoon ground coriander
- 1/2 teaspoon ground allspice
- 1/4 teaspoon cayenne pepper (optional, for heat)
- Salt and black pepper, to taste
- 2 cups chicken broth
- 2 large ripe plantains, peeled and cut into 1-inch pieces
- 1 cup frozen peas or green beans (optional)
- 1 tablespoon chopped fresh parsley or cilantro (for garnish)

Instructions:

1. **Prepare the Chicken:**
   - Season the chicken pieces with salt and black pepper.
   - Heat the oil in a large pot or Dutch oven over medium-high heat.
   - Add the chicken pieces and brown them on all sides, about 5-7 minutes. Remove the chicken from the pot and set aside.
2. **Prepare the Stew Base:**
   - In the same pot, add the chopped onion and cook for 3-4 minutes until softened.
   - Add the minced garlic and diced bell pepper, and cook for another 2 minutes until fragrant.
   - Stir in the diced tomatoes, tomato paste, paprika, ground cumin, dried thyme, ground coriander, ground allspice, and cayenne pepper (if using). Cook for 5 minutes, allowing the tomato paste to caramelize slightly.
3. **Cook the Stew:**
   - Return the browned chicken to the pot, along with any accumulated juices.
   - Pour in the chicken broth, making sure the chicken is mostly covered. Bring the stew to a simmer.
   - Cover the pot and cook for 20 minutes.
4. **Add Plantains and Vegetables:**
   - Add the plantain pieces to the pot. Continue to simmer, covered, for an additional 10-15 minutes, or until the plantains are tender and the chicken is fully cooked (internal temperature should reach 165°F or 74°C).
   - If using, add the frozen peas or green beans during the last 5 minutes of cooking.

5. **Finish and Serve:**
   - Check the seasoning and adjust with salt and black pepper as needed.
   - Garnish with chopped fresh parsley or cilantro.

Enjoy your Plantain and Chicken Stew, a hearty and flavorful dish that combines sweet plantains with savory chicken and aromatic spices!

Spicy Fish Tacos with Pineapple Slaw

Ingredients:

For the Spicy Fish:

- 1 lb (450g) firm white fish (such as cod, tilapia, or snapper), cut into strips
- 1/2 cup all-purpose flour
- 1/2 cup cornmeal
- 1 teaspoon smoked paprika
- 1/2 teaspoon ground cumin
- 1/2 teaspoon garlic powder
- 1/4 teaspoon cayenne pepper (optional, for extra heat)
- Salt and black pepper, to taste
- 1/2 cup buttermilk (or milk with 1 tablespoon lemon juice)
- Vegetable oil for frying

For the Pineapple Slaw:

- 2 cups shredded cabbage (green or a mix of green and red)
- 1 cup diced pineapple (fresh or canned)
- 1/2 cup shredded carrots
- 1/4 cup finely chopped red onion
- 1/4 cup chopped fresh cilantro
- 1/4 cup mayonnaise
- 2 tablespoons pineapple juice
- 1 tablespoon lime juice (about 1 lime)
- 1 tablespoon honey or agave syrup
- Salt and black pepper, to taste

For Assembly:

- 8 small tortillas (flour or corn)
- Lime wedges for serving
- Extra chopped cilantro for garnish (optional)

Instructions:

1. **Prepare the Pineapple Slaw:**
    - In a large bowl, combine shredded cabbage, diced pineapple, shredded carrots, finely chopped red onion, and chopped cilantro.
    - In a small bowl, whisk together mayonnaise, pineapple juice, lime juice, and honey or agave syrup.
    - Pour the dressing over the slaw mixture and toss to combine. Season with salt and black pepper to taste.
    - Refrigerate the slaw until ready to serve, allowing the flavors to meld.
2. **Prepare the Spicy Fish:**
    - In a shallow bowl, mix together flour, cornmeal, smoked paprika, ground cumin, garlic powder, cayenne pepper (if using), salt, and black pepper.

- Pour the buttermilk into another shallow bowl.
- Dip each fish strip into the buttermilk, allowing excess to drip off, then dredge in the flour mixture, pressing gently to adhere.
- Heat vegetable oil in a large skillet over medium-high heat. There should be enough oil to cover the bottom of the skillet.
- Fry the fish strips in batches, cooking for 2-3 minutes per side, or until golden brown and crispy. Transfer the cooked fish to a paper-towel-lined plate to drain.
3. **Assemble the Tacos:**
    - Warm the tortillas in a dry skillet or microwave until pliable.
    - Place a few pieces of fried fish in each tortilla.
    - Top with a generous amount of pineapple slaw.
4. **Serve:**
    - Garnish with extra chopped cilantro if desired.
    - Serve with lime wedges for squeezing over the tacos.

Enjoy your Spicy Fish Tacos with Pineapple Slaw, a perfect blend of spicy, crispy fish and refreshing, tangy slaw in every bite!

Jamaican Jerk Turkey Burgers

Ingredients:

For the Jerk Turkey Burgers:

- 1 lb (450g) ground turkey
- 2 tablespoons Jamaican jerk seasoning (store-bought or homemade)
- 1 tablespoon olive oil
- 1/2 cup finely chopped onion
- 2 cloves garlic, minced
- 1 tablespoon fresh thyme leaves (or 1 teaspoon dried thyme)
- 1/2 teaspoon allspice
- 1/2 teaspoon paprika
- 1/4 teaspoon cayenne pepper (optional, for extra heat)
- 1/4 cup breadcrumbs (optional, for binding)
- 1 egg (optional, for binding)
- Salt and black pepper, to taste

For Serving:

- 4 hamburger buns
- Lettuce leaves
- Sliced tomato
- Sliced red onion
- Sliced avocado (optional)
- Mango chutney or a jerk sauce (optional)

Instructions:

1. **Prepare the Turkey Mixture:**
   - In a large bowl, combine ground turkey, Jamaican jerk seasoning, olive oil, finely chopped onion, minced garlic, fresh thyme leaves, allspice, paprika, and cayenne pepper (if using).
   - If using breadcrumbs and egg, add them to the mixture to help bind the burgers together.
   - Season with salt and black pepper to taste.
   - Mix gently until all ingredients are combined, being careful not to overmix.
2. **Form the Patties:**
   - Divide the mixture into 4 equal portions and shape each portion into a patty, about 3/4-inch thick.
3. **Cook the Patties:**
   - Heat a grill or grill pan to medium-high heat. Lightly oil the grill grates or pan.
   - Cook the patties for 5-7 minutes per side, or until they are fully cooked through and reach an internal temperature of 165°F (74°C).
4. **Assemble the Burgers:**
   - Toast the hamburger buns on the grill or in a toaster if desired.
   - Place a cooked turkey patty on the bottom half of each bun.
   - Top with lettuce, sliced tomato, sliced red onion, and avocado if using.
   - Add a dollop of mango chutney or jerk sauce if desired.
   - Place the top half of the bun on the burger.

5. **Serve:**
    - Serve the burgers immediately, garnished with extra jerk sauce or mango chutney on the side if desired.

Enjoy your Jamaican Jerk Turkey Burgers, a spicy and flavorful twist on a classic favorite that's sure to impress!

Pineapple and Mango Chicken Skewers

Ingredients:

For the Marinade:

- 1/2 cup pineapple juice (fresh or canned)

- 1/4 cup mango juice (or use additional pineapple juice)
- 2 tablespoons soy sauce (or tamari for gluten-free)
- 2 tablespoons honey or agave syrup
- 2 tablespoons lime juice (about 1 lime)
- 1 tablespoon grated fresh ginger
- 2 cloves garlic, minced
- 1 teaspoon ground cumin
- 1/2 teaspoon smoked paprika
- 1/4 teaspoon ground cayenne pepper (optional, for extra heat)
- Salt and black pepper, to taste

For the Skewers:

- 1.5 lbs (680g) boneless, skinless chicken breasts or thighs, cut into 1-inch cubes
- 1 cup fresh pineapple chunks
- 1 cup fresh mango chunks
- 1 red bell pepper, cut into 1-inch pieces
- 1 green bell pepper, cut into 1-inch pieces
- 1 small red onion, cut into 1-inch pieces
- Fresh cilantro for garnish (optional)

Instructions:

1. **Prepare the Marinade:**
    - In a medium bowl, whisk together pineapple juice, mango juice, soy sauce, honey or agave syrup, lime juice, grated ginger, minced garlic, ground cumin, smoked paprika, and cayenne pepper (if using).
    - Season with salt and black pepper to taste.
2. **Marinate the Chicken:**
    - Place the chicken cubes in a large resealable plastic bag or a bowl.
    - Pour half of the marinade over the chicken, reserving the other half for basting.
    - Seal the bag or cover the bowl and refrigerate for at least 30 minutes, or up to 4 hours for more flavor.
3. **Prepare the Skewers:**
    - If using wooden skewers, soak them in water for at least 30 minutes to prevent burning.
    - Preheat the grill to medium-high heat.
    - Thread the marinated chicken, pineapple chunks, mango chunks, bell peppers, and red onion onto the skewers, alternating as desired.
4. **Grill the Skewers:**
    - Lightly oil the grill grates to prevent sticking.
    - Place the skewers on the grill and cook for about 10-12 minutes, turning occasionally, until the chicken is cooked through and reaches an internal temperature of 165°F (74°C). Baste with the reserved marinade during the last few minutes of grilling.

5. **Serve:**
    - Remove the skewers from the grill and let them rest for a few minutes.
    - Garnish with fresh cilantro if desired.

Enjoy your Pineapple and Mango Chicken Skewers, a delightful and tropical dish perfect for summer grilling or any time you want a taste of the tropics!

Tropical Black Bean Soup

Ingredients:

For the Soup:

- 2 tablespoons olive oil

- 1 large onion, finely chopped
- 2 cloves garlic, minced
- 1 red bell pepper, diced
- 1 green bell pepper, diced
- 2 teaspoons ground cumin
- 1 teaspoon smoked paprika
- 1/2 teaspoon ground coriander
- 1/2 teaspoon dried oregano
- 1/4 teaspoon cayenne pepper (optional, for heat)
- 1 can (15 oz) black beans, drained and rinsed
- 1 can (15 oz) diced tomatoes (with juice)
- 1 cup vegetable or chicken broth
- 1 cup coconut milk (canned)
- 1 cup fresh pineapple chunks (or canned, drained)
- 1 tablespoon lime juice (about 1 lime)
- Salt and black pepper, to taste

For Garnish (optional):

- Fresh cilantro, chopped
- Sliced green onions
- Diced avocado
- Lime wedges
- Crumbled tortilla chips

Instructions:

1. **Prepare the Soup Base:**
   - Heat olive oil in a large pot over medium heat.
   - Add the chopped onion and cook for 3-4 minutes, until softened.
   - Add the minced garlic and cook for another 1 minute, until fragrant.
   - Stir in the diced red and green bell peppers, and cook for 3-4 minutes, until they start to soften.
2. **Add Spices and Beans:**
   - Stir in the ground cumin, smoked paprika, ground coriander, dried oregano, and cayenne pepper (if using). Cook for 1 minute to toast the spices.
   - Add the black beans, diced tomatoes (with juice), and vegetable or chicken broth. Bring to a simmer.
3. **Simmer the Soup:**
   - Reduce the heat to low and let the soup simmer for about 10-15 minutes, allowing the flavors to meld.
4. **Add Coconut and Pineapple:**
   - Stir in the coconut milk and fresh pineapple chunks. Continue to simmer for an additional 5 minutes, until heated through and the pineapple is slightly softened.
5. **Finish and Serve:**

- Stir in the lime juice and season with salt and black pepper to taste.
- Serve the soup hot, garnished with fresh cilantro, sliced green onions, diced avocado, lime wedges, and crumbled tortilla chips if desired.

Enjoy your Tropical Black Bean Soup, a comforting and flavorful dish with a tropical twist that's perfect for any time of year!

Grilled Fish Sandwiches with Mango Chutney

Ingredients:

For the Fish:

- 1 lb (450g) firm white fish fillets (such as cod, tilapia, or snapper)

- 2 tablespoons olive oil
- 1 teaspoon smoked paprika
- 1/2 teaspoon garlic powder
- 1/2 teaspoon onion powder
- 1/2 teaspoon dried oregano
- 1/4 teaspoon cayenne pepper (optional, for heat)
- Salt and black pepper, to taste
- 1 tablespoon fresh lemon juice (about 1 lemon)

For the Mango Chutney:

- 1 ripe mango, peeled and diced
- 1/4 cup finely chopped red onion
- 1/4 cup chopped fresh cilantro
- 1 tablespoon lime juice (about 1 lime)
- 1 tablespoon honey or agave syrup
- 1/2 teaspoon grated fresh ginger
- 1 small chili pepper, finely chopped (optional, for heat)
- Salt to taste

For the Sandwiches:

- 4 hamburger buns or sandwich rolls
- Lettuce leaves
- Sliced tomato
- Sliced red onion
- Pickles (optional)

Instructions:

1. **Prepare the Mango Chutney:**
   - In a medium bowl, combine diced mango, finely chopped red onion, chopped cilantro, lime juice, honey or agave syrup, grated ginger, and chopped chili pepper (if using).
   - Mix well and season with salt to taste.
   - Set aside to allow the flavors to meld.
2. **Prepare the Fish:**
   - Preheat the grill to medium-high heat.
   - In a small bowl, mix together olive oil, smoked paprika, garlic powder, onion powder, dried oregano, cayenne pepper (if using), salt, and black pepper.
   - Rub the spice mixture over the fish fillets.
   - Drizzle the fish with fresh lemon juice.
3. **Grill the Fish:**
   - Lightly oil the grill grates to prevent sticking.

- Grill the fish fillets for about 3-4 minutes per side, or until the fish is cooked through and flakes easily with a fork.
- Remove from the grill and let rest for a few minutes.
4. **Assemble the Sandwiches:**
    - Toast the hamburger buns or sandwich rolls on the grill or in a toaster if desired.
    - Place a grilled fish fillet on the bottom half of each bun.
    - Top with a generous spoonful of mango chutney.
    - Add lettuce leaves, sliced tomato, sliced red onion, and pickles if desired.
    - Place the top half of the bun on the sandwich.
5. **Serve:**
    - Serve the sandwiches immediately while the fish is still warm and the buns are toasted.

Enjoy your Grilled Fish Sandwiches with Mango Chutney, a fresh and vibrant meal perfect for a summer lunch or dinner!

Caribbean Chicken and Pineapple Stir-Fry

Ingredients:

For the Stir-Fry:

- 1 lb (450g) boneless, skinless chicken breasts or thighs, thinly sliced
- 2 tablespoons vegetable oil or coconut oil
- 1 red bell pepper, sliced
- 1 green bell pepper, sliced
- 1 cup fresh pineapple chunks (or canned, drained)
- 1 medium carrot, thinly sliced
- 1 small onion, sliced
- 2 cloves garlic, minced
- 1 teaspoon fresh ginger, minced
- 1/4 cup chopped fresh cilantro (optional, for garnish)
- Cooked rice or noodles, for serving

For the Caribbean Sauce:

- 1/4 cup soy sauce (or tamari for gluten-free)
- 1/4 cup pineapple juice
- 2 tablespoons brown sugar or honey
- 2 tablespoons rice vinegar or apple cider vinegar
- 1 tablespoon cornstarch mixed with 2 tablespoons water (for thickening)
- 1 teaspoon allspice
- 1/2 teaspoon ground cumin
- 1/4 teaspoon cayenne pepper (optional, for heat)

Instructions:

1. **Prepare the Sauce:**
   - In a small bowl, whisk together soy sauce, pineapple juice, brown sugar or honey, rice vinegar, allspice, ground cumin, and cayenne pepper (if using).
   - Mix the cornstarch with water to make a slurry, then stir it into the sauce mixture.
   - Set aside.
2. **Cook the Chicken:**
   - Heat the oil in a large skillet or wok over medium-high heat.
   - Add the sliced chicken and cook for 5-7 minutes, or until the chicken is cooked through and starting to brown. Remove the chicken from the skillet and set aside.
3. **Stir-Fry the Vegetables:**
   - In the same skillet, add a little more oil if needed.
   - Add the sliced onion, bell peppers, and carrots. Stir-fry for 3-4 minutes, or until the vegetables are tender-crisp.
   - Add the minced garlic and ginger, and stir-fry for an additional 1 minute.
4. **Combine and Finish:**
   - Return the cooked chicken to the skillet with the vegetables.
   - Add the pineapple chunks and pour the prepared sauce over everything.
   - Stir to combine and cook for another 2-3 minutes, until the sauce has thickened and everything is well-coated.
5. **Serve:**

- - Garnish with chopped fresh cilantro if desired.
  - Serve the stir-fry over cooked rice or noodles.

Enjoy your Caribbean Chicken and Pineapple Stir-Fry, a colorful and flavorful dish that brings a taste of the tropics to your table!

www.ingramcontent.com/pod-product-compliance
Lightning Source LLC
LaVergne TN
LVHW081600060526
838201LV00054B/1993